Nature and Nostalgia in the Poetry of Nader Naderpour

Nature and Nostalgia in the Poetry of Nader Naderpour

Rouhollah Zarei and Roger Sedarat

CAMBRIA
PRESS

Amherst, New York

Copyright 2017 Cambria Press.

All rights reserved.
Printed in the United States of America

No part of this publication may be reproduced, stored in or introduced into a retrieval system, or transmitted, in any form, or by any means (electronic, mechanical, photocopying, recording, or otherwise), without the prior permission of the publisher.

Requests for permission should be directed to
permissions@cambriapress.com, or mailed to:
Cambria Press
University Corporate Centre
100 Corporate Parkway, Suite 128
Amherst, New York 14226, USA

Cover image: Tree of Life pure Silk Qum Persian Rug woven in Qum IRAN. Ordered by tableaurug.com. Treasure Gallery Inc.

Library of Congress Cataloging-in-Publication Data

Names: Zarei, Rouhollah author. | Sedarat, Roger, 1971- author.

Title: Nature and nostalgia in the poetry of Nader Naderpour / Rouhollah Zarei and Roger Sedarat.

Description: Amherst, New York : Cambria Press, 2017. | Includes bibliographical references and index.

Identifiers: LCCN 2017004648 | ISBN 9781621963783 (alk. paper)

Subjects: LCSH: Neadirpeur, Neadir--Criticism and interpretation. | Nature in literature. | Nostalgia in literature.

Classification: LCC PK6561.N3 Z85 2017 | DDC 891/.5513--dc23
LC record available at https://lccn.loc.gov/2017004648

Cambria Press gratefully acknowledges the permission of Negah Publishers to publish these translations.

Table of Contents

Epigraph vii

Preface ix

Chapter 1: Naderpour: A Critical Study 1

Chapter 2: Nature 13

Chapter 3: Nature and Nostalgia 61

Chapter 4: Poet of Pictures 101

Chapter 5: Literary Translation in Modern Times 109

Epilogue 119

Bibliography 123

Epigraph

The Unsaid

There is a poem in my heart,
a poem of fire
consuming its own words,
a poem of rancor, rage, and revenge
that no one hears.
There is a poem in my heart,
a poem of a picture
escaping the frame,
a poem of inspiration
that I fail to write.
There is a poem in my heart,
a poem of love
resisting surrender,
a poem of the moment
written in the past. (*Blood and Ashes,* Tehran, April 25, 1954)

Preface

There are many modern Iranian poets who have been translated and introduced to Western readers. Some have had the chance to be retranslated. However, there are, as is always the case with poets from foreign traditions, many who remain relatively unknown. The present authors of this book believe the Nobel Prize nominee, Nader Naderpour (1929–2000), who, though he lived and taught in the US, warrants greater recognition in the English-speaking world. He was a poet whose romantic sensitivities are unforgettable for many Iranian readers. Because his poems were written over the course of decades and cover a variety of subjects, it is hard to pigeonhole him in just one school of poetry or one generation of poets. Based on his style and subjects, he occupies a place between traditional and modern poetry of Iran. However, his universal themes of nature, romance, and the passage of time (youth, old age, and death) ultimately can make his verse transnationally relatable.

While alive, there had been only one book on Naderpour in English, *False Dawn: Persian Poems by Nader Naderpour* (1986) by Professor Michael Craig Hillmann. At the time of his death, the poetry from his last books (arguably his best) had yet to come out. As co-translators and scholars well familiar with his works, we had a sense that together we could effectively access his style and meaning in our English renderings. Given the plethora of so many fine poems, selecting representative ones from each book proved rather difficult. Though we have made but a little headway here, we hope that our translations and brief scholarly overviews lead to further investigations and may pave the way for the publication of all of Naderpour's poems in one volume for the lovers of modern Persian poetry.

Nature and Nostalgia in the Poetry of Nader Naderpour

CHAPTER 1

NADERPOUR: A CRITICAL STUDY

Nima Yushij, pen name for Ali Esfandyari (1896–1960), can be considered the founder of modern Persian poetry. He broke away from the constraints of Persian prosodic measures and thus brought about a revolution in classical poetry. He set aside the traditional fixed-length hemistich and the rhyme while making an effort to adapt the language of poetry with the needs of contemporary life. Among his famous followers were Ahmad Shamlou, Mehdi Akhavan-Sales, Forough Farrokhzad, and Fereydoun Moshiri. The last was a conciliator of classical Persian poetry with the New Poetry. In this respect, Nader Naderpour occupies a similar place in modern Persian poetry. During a lecture at UCLA in 1989 for the commemoration of Naderpour's 60th birthday, Ehsan Yarshater, the founder and director of the Center for Iranian Studies, maintained: "If I were to inhabit a (deserted) island and take a collection of a contemporary poet, I would have gone with Naderpour although no collection of him is published, I would have been happy with at least a selection of his poems" (Eidgah 297).

Naderpour's evolution as a poet was steady and consistent over decades of literary activity. In the 1950s he was already well-known, but the 1960s marked the pinnacle of fame. In the 1970s his poetry revolutionized and became more intellectual, with new horizons opening before him. He used transparent, contemporary diction and lucid imagery influenced by both French Romantics as well as the eleventh-century Persian poet Manouchehri Damghani, who is renowned for his pictorial description of nature. Insofar as he connected the classical to the new Persian movement, a modern Iranian critic called him "the hinge" (Hoqouqi, *Poetry* 382). Manouchehr Atashi, a contemporary poet, believes that he got eloquence from classical Persian poetry and his sensibility from Yushij, avoiding the latter's deconstructionism (Salahshour 49). Importantly, he kept away from boring repetitions and the pitfalls of the commonplace that are the enemies of art. Unlike some poets of the New Poetry movement, he was eloquent, coherent, and musical, with new combinations and similes, full of novel and enchanting themes.

The term "hinge" remains especially apt, considering how other critics have typified him: "neo-romantic" (Farzan 342), "semi-traditionalist" (Zarghani 336), "moderate" (Shafi'ee 130), "the great ideologue of youth and maturity" (Roya'ee, *Absent-mindedness* 181) or "clairvoyant" (Roya'ee, *Contemplating* 217), and "a modern classic of Persian literature" (Yarshater, "A Star" 153). Overall, Naderpour was the representative of his age. That is why Karimi-Hakkak calls him "the most emulated poet" (Mozaffari 395).

The tumultuous modern world in which Naderpour lived in part accounts for his aesthetic. Leonardo Alishan, discussing the collection *False Dawn*, examines Naderpour's worldview in this light:

> The roots of chronological wandering must be sought in Naderpour's chaotic worldview. He was born in unfavorable times. On the one hand, his deep knowledge of classic Persian culture and poetry draw him to an orderly, secure and spiritual worldview and on the other hand his rebellious soul, concurring with European and especially French poets of the late nineteenth century who rebelled against heavenly and earthly gods, pulls him away from such concepts.... In the former worldview death is the beginning, marriage with God, but as Naderpour is godless he is afraid of old

age and death and cannot adapt himself with the transient earthly life.... If Naderpour finds God or abandons looking for Him for good there will be fewer contradictions and more depth, strength and maturity in his poems. If however he hovers between this unstable state of being with God at times and godless at other times, we will witness more clashes of sorrow of old age with the passion of youth. (Alishan 352–8)

Two prominent features of Naderpour's poetry, refined language and his unique imagery, have transformed him into an unforgettable poet for his and the present generation of readers.

A SHORT AUTOBIOGRAPHY

"I was born on 6th June, 1929, in Tehran. My parents were relatives, both descendants of noble and aristocratic lineage. They not only understood ancient and modern Persian literature and culture and were quite familiar with French culture and language but also loved the twin arts of painting and music. My father painted and my mother played musical instruments skillfully. At the age of five, two years before formally starting school, I learned the Persian alphabet from my father because he made me read *Iran*, the only morning paper of the time every evening at his bed. My father encouraged me to recite and memorize poems by Ghââni, Farrokhi Sistani and Manouchehri. Thus, my interest in Persian poetry grew and gradually I was introduced to ancient and modern Persian poetry. My interest in music and painting was no less than literature. When one rainy day in the spring I was going back home from school, I met laughing passers-by who still had drops of rain on their faces. I composed the following lines that after sixty years are still fresh:

> The cool gentle breeze is blowing from every side
> The sky is shedding tears of joy on people's faces.

The great change took place in me at the age of 14, about a year after the occupation of Iran by the Allies. The sudden attack put an end to the heroic feelings that had enchanted my coevals and me (owing to the massive state propaganda as well as splendid parades of soldiers on every February 22)[1] towards the end of Reza Shah's reign. Instead, we were overwhelmed by angry and painful moods to which, in my childish world, only poetry could give expression. Thus, I put aside all painting and musical activities and composed poems only and soon I became skillful in it.

I used to buy *Sokhan* (*Speech*), a literary magazine, regularly and read avidly poems by the late Shahriar or the late Dr. Mahdi Hamidi Shirazi and other masters of modern Persian poetry. Another factor that helped me improve on and modernize my poetry was French, the treasure I inherited from my knowledgeable and cultivated parents. I started to study French poetry and soon I was familiar with Charles Baudelaire. Putting together what I had learned from French and modern Persian poetry, I managed to compose "Dance of the Dead" with a short introduction by Ehsan Tabari. It was followed by "A Night in Farmlands" and "A Madman" in *Mardom* (*People*) monthly in 1947. That was the beginning of my career, which has continued thriving ever since. In 1950, after getting my diploma, I went to Paris to study French language and literature and thus I had the opportunity to study ancient and modern French poets and to translate some of them into Persian including Rimbaud, Baudelaire, Verlaine, and Valéry. They were published before the revolution in literary magazines like *Sokhan* monthly. In addition, I went to Italy to study Italian language and literature, the result was the translation of seven modern Italian poets into Persian in a book co-authored by a young friend Bijan Oshidari titled *Seven Portraits of Contemporary Italian Poets* by the former Franklin Publishing Institute.

After graduating and returning home, I published my first collection of poems, *Eyes and Hands* (1954). Six more collections, including *Daughter of the Cup* (1955), *The Grapes Poem* (1958), *The Sun's Kohl* (1960) followed and in 1979 I published three volumes of *Not Plant and Stone but Fire*, *From the Sublime to the Ridiculous*, and *The Last Supper*. They went into subsequent editions, the last of which was in 1980. However, none has been republished in Iran for twenty years and I hope some Iranian in the US will publish them in one or two volumes." (Naderpour, *Persian Heritage* 114–117)

A Short Chronology

1929	Born on June 6 in Tehran
1942–1948	Iranshahr High School, studied art appreciation, music, and French.
1950	entered Sorbonne University to study French literature
1954	*Eyes and Hands (Chashmhâ va Dasthâ)* his first volume of poems,
1955	*Daughter of the Cup (Dokhtare Jâm)* his second collection of poems,
1958	*The Grapes Poem (Shere Angûr)* his third collection of poems,
1960	*Kohl of the Sun (Sormeye Khorshid)*
1964	travelled to Italy to study Italian language and literature
1968	a founding member of the Association of Iranian Writers.
1977	left the Association. Became the director of "Gorûhe Adabe Emrûz" ("Eve of Today's Literature") on Iranian National Radio and Television.
1978	*Not Plant and Stone, But Fire (Giyâh-o Sang na, Âtash)*
1978	*From the Sublime to the Ridiculous (Az Âsemân ta Rismân)*
1978	*The Last Supper (Shâme Bâz Pasin)*
1980	Naderpour moved to Paris after the Islamic revolution
1982	*False Dawn (Sobhe Dorûghin)* published in Paris and later on in Los Angeles, which includes poems composed during 1978–1982
1984	married his compatriot, Jaleh Basiri
1986	moved to the United States and lectured at universities including Harvard University, Georgetown University, UC Berkeley, UCLA, UCI.

1989	*Blood and Ashes (Khûn-o Khâkestar)* published in Los Angeles
1993	nominated for the Nobel Prize in Literature. Recipient of the Lillian Hellman and Dashiell Hammett Prize
1996	*Earth and Time (Zamin-o Zamân)* published in the US
1998	the Ehsan Yarshater Award, conferred by the Roudaki Cultural Foundation
2000	died in his Los Angeles home on February 18

NADERPOUR ON POETRY

Throughout his prolific life, Naderpour wrote much about poetry. We have attempted to provide a general picture of his views on literature and poetry in particular, choosing passages from Naderpour's writings that might best prove of interest to an English-speaking reader. In 1961, Naderpour in an essay, "New or Old," commented on the novelty and imitation. He maintained:

> To venerate ancient masters of poetry is not to imitate them word for word, "inelegantly" spoiling their labor and with boring repetition reducing their nuances and novelties to the commonplace. This is a daytime robbery and a looting of what they earned from the deep recesses of their memories or of nature's treasury. Instead, one should, while respecting their "copyright" and their dignity, use them as models rather than "scribing" their poems. This demands a will and power which is not to be found in everybody.... All real poets in their times have been original and have borne the anger of "worshippers of the ancient" and have accepted the excommunication of traditionalists. (Eidgah 32–33).

OLD AND NEW POETRY

Naderpour accepted Nima's ground-breaking proposition to change the equal length of poetry lines, respecting instead the needs of conversational speech. That is, in conversation lines have different length and patterns based on one's purpose. The same rule can govern poetry as emotions and thoughts are not necessarily expressed in equal lengths. He also agreed with Nima's two other suggestions according to which a poem should not be imprisoned in a single meter; rather, it could be comprised of a number of homogenous meters. In addition, the rhyme does not need to appear in final position (Naderpour, *Persian Heritage*, 117).

In Naderpour's eyes, new poetry needs a new conception. A poet need not describe inventions like trains or airplanes in order to make poetry new. It is unnecessary to use foreign words or a purified Persian lexicon but one should see the world through one's own eyes. One should abandon other clichéd metaphors, like the full moon for the description of the beloved's face, for example, or a bow for the eyebrow (Salahshour 122).

Naderpour argued that the vision and conception of ancient poets were often narrow. For instance, the classical poet could not write of his quarrel with his wife, as that would deviate from social etiquette and canon laws. Also, the literary conventions of the time allowed only for a certain type of diction into poetry (Salahshour 123). Naderpour came up with an example to exemplify his claim for modern expression from his contemporary Fereydoun Tavallali:

> My wife shouts from a corner:
> "Man, stop it now!
> With the two kids of yours, you are no spring chicken;
> put aside lust at this old age."

Naderpour believed that while poets of the past expressed their emotions indirectly and wrapped them in simple natural imagery, today the poet is explicit and direct. This view of Naderpour of course remains open to criticism because many critics and poets, in Iran and in other traditions, believe that the beauty of poetry is in its indirectness of expression. The etymology of the word 'verse' in Latin is of help in this regard. Reza Barahani pointed to some bad examples of direct method in Naderpour and maintained that they are simply philosophy not poetry (Barahani 62–63).

Naderpour believed that another factor responsible for the rise of the new poetry in Iran was the direct or indirect influence of European literature. The influence started with inaccurate translations of European works, and the French language, which had been the language of the aristocracy in Iran and then became that of the middle class; besides, travels added to the spread of Western literature. Naderpour admitted that the influences, both harmful and useful, were undeniable. The share of French literature was greater than others in this matter (Salahshour 126).

To Naderpour new poetry was the spiritual need of modern times, though it had origins in material circumstances (Salahshour 128). Thus, only new poetry could meet the spiritual needs of the modern age. According to Naderpour, the poet was not a creator but a discoverer. The poem in the depth of the psyche was like oil deep down beneath the earth. The poet drilled a well and reached some streams of oil (Salahshour 131). The new poetry should have new outlook and a new texture (Salahshour 137).

Sound and Sense

Naderpour maintained that he was the poet of his generation. He did not see and want the language isolated from the content. Therefore, he put forth what he felt in the current language. His language was not so complicated as to scare the reader away, nor was it so simple as to bore the elite. For this reason, he has had readers from among the general readership as well as the elites. "Form and content" he asserted, "like twins are born together" (Eidgah 186). Elsewhere, in "The Two Pans of Sound and Sense on the Scales of Poetry" (1989) he proposed that one of the basic signs of good poetry is the balance of the sound and sense on its scales, something which is not possible all the time (Eidgah 40). He believed that recent years have been impregnated with ample meaning and have been the richest periods of poetry and thus sense has been outweighing sound (Eidgah 50). He enumerated three reasons poetasters employ the word in the most inappropriate place and confuse the reader:

1. They might have a more or less strong sensibility but weak expression and because of little or no knowledge of Persian letters among those who do not have mastery over words.
2. If they have mediocre sensibility, their expression is at the same level and thus two mediocre things will not produce anything good.
3. If they have a mediocre sensibility, or none at all, they intentionally complicate the expression lest the reader should come to know about the emptiness of their heads or hearts. They are charlatans who cheat customers at their "Poetry Shops." They do not know (or know well enough) that Persian poetry has proved that a competent poet expresses the most complicated meanings in the simplest and clearest language. (Eidgah 61)

Naderpour continued that poetry or any other art is not an inborn talent but will remain incomplete if unaided by skill (or technique). He came up with the metaphor that poetry is not the rain that pours down, but the elixir for whose production not only the material but also the knowledge would be needed. Talent is inborn but technique is acquired. Therefore, learning the skill is not a fault or sin but a virtue and duty. The skill is like the body of the poem. If a body is unhealthy, the soul will likewise suffer. The modern poet is in need of technique even more than the ancients since new concepts demand new techniques of expression. Therefore, the poet should learn the ancient poetical techniques, modernize, and utilize them according to new circumstances (Eidgah 67–8).

The Poet: The Personal and Universal

Roya'ee saw Naderpour as a visionary poet by coming up with examples from "A Dream to Wakefulness," "False Dawn," and "The Last Supper." He maintained, "The prediction and discovery of future events usually happens in visionary poets. When they isolate themselves from the world around them, they are able to watch the world free from the passage of the world. They dream of the cosmos" (Roya'ee, "Contemplating" 217). Naderpour not only isolated himself from the world around him but also, like the Romantic writers, divided his personality into two halves to better reach the clairvoyance that many people had already witnessed in him. He observed:

> When I compose a poem, my personality divides into two parts; one is me, and the other a meddlesome, importunate, exigent, and invisible person who sits by me and fights over my catch. Sometimes he is happy (and that is the moment I feel complacent) and sometimes looks grouchy although I am happier and prouder than ever with my productions. However, his complaining looks makes me set aside personal satisfaction to please this intrusive but dear being as this is of more importance to me. I have called this being, "people's representative." I have been in perpetual agreement with him. As soon as I start a poem, I see this kind person sitting by me who is appointed by his constituents to check me. Despite his strong defense on behalf of his constituents, I have never sacrificed all my personality, even the half belonging to me, to people's expectations and understanding. (qtd. in Roya'ee, *Absent-mindedness* 233–234)

Roya'ee continues that he has witnessed that "people's representative" in every poem by Naderpour; however, the people are not unified so at times he has been pleasing himself and the elite and at other times the reverse (Roya'ee, *Absent-mindedness* 234).

Notes

1. The anniversary of Reza Shah's (at that time Reza Khan's) victorious but bloodless coup d'état on February 22, 1921 during which he along with Sayyed Ziaoddin Tabatabai took control of the government that was previously in the hands of Ahmad Shah, the last king of Qajar dynasty.

Chapter 2

Nature

Naderpour is hailed as a love poet in Iran. Despite the influence of other modern writers and the contemporary evolution of society, there were several factors to give him impetus to write in a romantic mode. In the same way that social revolutions had a great share in the formation of the Romantic movement in Europe, so did the constitutional Revolution in Iran (1905–1907) bring about changes in different walks of life, including literature. The spread of urbanization reminded the poet of the gradual loss of direct contact with nature which, up until then, had been going unnoticed owing to its proximity and familiarity. A poet like Naderpour who was born in the large capital of the country had sufficient motivation to see life from a natural perspective. Thus, a yearning for the return to nature is perceptible in many of his poems. While *Daughter of the Cup* has the least references to nature with just one poem, *Not Plant and Stone but Fire*, has 32 poems on the theme. Overall, about a third of Naderpour's poems bear on nature, a remarkable indication of his emotional and intellectual mindset.

Direct contact with Western literature was another main factor familiarizing Iranians with the latest literary movements in Europe. Students were sent to be educated in Europe; books were read in French (the intellectual language of the time among Iranians), or were translated from French, Russian, and English into Persian. It is obvious that Romanticism as a revolutionary movement belonging to middle class society did not find audiences in classical-minded people. A similar situation was prevalent in Persian literature. The classic rules, subjects, genres, and even imagery were already set. Any change in these patterns was an unpardonable sin.

However, the New Poetry movement in Iran broke away from the established metrical and rhyme patterns. It also updated the reservoir of subjects by introducing subjects that met the need of a twentieth-century Iranian. As Shams Langroudi maintained, "Naderpour's moderate and neo-classical poetry attracted most audiences in the 1950s because of the romantic and living images, addressing deep sensibilities and anxieties in modern human beings, and the ease and fluency of language" (Langroudi, 1370, vol. 2, 57).

NATURE: THE CITY AND THE COUNTRY

For Naderpour, city life is the product of new civilization, and warranting interrogation and criticism. He sees the city as "darker than coffins," the air "full of blood and gun powder" and love "morbid."

> A Migration Song
>
> The red bow of twilight
> sliced a raven groove on the blue arms of trees
> as a nest opened its mouth like an infected wound.
>
> Someone brought news of the city:
> the houses darker than coffins[1]
> the air permeated with the smell of blood and powder,
> gunmen's torches burning smoke and laughter,
> no drunkards exiled to alleyways,
> no wind through the leaves.

Nature

Someone brought news from the city:
all loves turned morbid,
all windows: feverish eyes
watching in dreams,
swallows danced in the spring sky
recalling humans swinging from the gallows,
foundations of their houses built on the executioner's block.

Someone brought news from the city:
the massacre of carpet flowers
with muddy boots,
the mirror consigning the keen power of memory
to premature dotage,
and from above the clay bricks of the city walls
the moon sees its vacant reflection

as it approaches to rub its wet cheeks
against dark blue windowpanes.
The lamp says
there is no one in the dark of a waiting corridor,
it is the distant whispering of specters
coming from within the hall
and the night brings the news from the garden that Cloud, the goldsmith,
no longer cuts dewdrop stones
to lay at on the trembling fingers of leaves
beside the marriage of flowers at dawn.

And the wind says
no leaves on trees will remain
so the tree will forget the magic of dancing:
standing naked by the brook,
arms stretched toward heaven in prayer
to beg for a penny
from that dishonorable rich man.
The earth is entirely dark
and no light plays on water

and will not be reflected on the sky's dome.
Pack your vacation luggage
and face another beach!
lest in the wasteful night of exile
your sorrows should drop tear seeds on the ground.... (*Not Plant,*
Paris January 5, 1966)

The Museum

Look at those who pass by in the city!
Look at the young and the old:
Stone from their waists to their heads
and the rest of them skin and veins.
They keep in motion, but with legs limping, eyes blind, and tongues dumb.
The city, this dark colossal museum,
is full of these statues:
heads dead, legs alive,
half of their bodies still
and the other half moving,
the city ridiculous from their comings and goings. (*From the Sublime*, Tehran, March 1967)

An Elegy for Desert and City

1

The earth has forgotten
the mercy of rain in small springs,
and the wind has blown out the red lights
on wild and sour orange trees
in pathways of the forest.
From a distance, disturbed hills
shout out the ruthlessness of time,
and gold lizards in narrow holes,
like the earth's tongue,
complain with the wind.

Nature

Ravens, waiting for winter on dry treetops,
chew the bit of snow on the Alborz peak
with their eyes.
Perplexed spiders, deprived of weaving,
wander among weeds.

Playful young sparrows nest
in lacerations on ancient trees.
Blood and pride season the bread
in travelers' insignificant backpacks.

2

In the city
doors and archways stand only as tall
as the short men.
No woman raises her head
from behind a window.
Frenetic need has removed the callus
once so visible on the forehead
of the praying man.
The tap of fear on window panes
disturbs children's dreams
and occasionally the rain
washes away traces of blood
into drain pipes.

Men have enclosed their dead hearts
in small vials of alcohol
and girls store their affection
in powder boxes.
Friendship has no meaning;
People have forgotten each other's languages.
A host of migrating words
without permission to pass
travel from borders toward printing houses,
and sob,
this mouthful, too big for the throat,

has filled the hunger pit,
wetting dry bread with tears.
Children's energy has run,
morning to evening,
in alleyways of mischief
and on rooftops,
waiting to ambush pigeons

and blind the eyes
of street lamps with stones.

The sun and the moon,
red and yellow balloons,
fly in the vacant sky
and days and nights,
these counterfeit coins,
rub off in dirty hands.

The laughter of flowers
no longer inspires windows;
singing no longer comes from vocal cords.
Cigarettes, between fingers,
have long replaced pens
and addictive smoke
has darkened both hearts and houses.
A man, out of his wife's sight,
longing to win the game,
loses his ace of hearts
and a woman who paints
incessantly repeats her picture
in the mirror's frame.
Placing paper flowers and artificial fruits
in pots and containers
she loves "Still Life."

3

In city and desert
the devil claims absolute dominion;

in the sun
no sound but crickets
cursing the wind with their stuttering.
The absence of clear voices
except from passers-by in alleyways
occasionally starting an old song
with these incomplete lines:
"Absent hope!
isn't it time to come?
Though the stone of revolt in your hand
is almost too heavy to hold,
Perhaps it will still hit
the distant target?" (*Not Plant,* Sorrento, August 4, 1965)

In "City and Night" consider how human beings are dwarfed before skyscrapers:

City and Night

Tonight the hungry on the earth have stolen
the loaf of moon from the tablecloth of the sea's bounty
but the drunken breeze
at the time of shaking this extended cloth
has given away the shining pictures of thousands of stars
like crusts of bread
to fish both big and small
and they have honored the breeze for benevolence.
Tonight along horizons and waves
night has slid down the city's shoulders
and now the lids of windows open
like black cats in a dark well opening their amber eyes.

Tonight the earthly god, in imitation of the galaxy
discloses a city full of stars,
his miraculous raising a hundred skyscrapers in the dark
as fast as a shout
to herald the rising of the moon.
They have opened doors
on the evening's horizons:

one in the form of a beehive
the other like an ebony chess box
and another one as a home refrigerator
and from the dark and lit cells of each
like an unskilled thief
they glance around with fear and wonder.
If a viewer looks up
from the latches of these sinister castles
he feels that the sky robs him of the hat
on his perplexed head.
If he looks down:
he will come to know that the miserable human body,
under the lamp, is a nail half-driven
into the crossroads' luminous chest.[2]
And if he looks at a distance
the tall palm tree on the beach
becomes a naked child
who has left gossamer bed
and has taken refuge in the evening
from a nightmare.

Here human dignity and the tree's height,
shrink in embarrassment
before the dignified skyscraper.
Here gold's footsteps go to heaven
to save the sun from going astray.
Here the door of a heart's house is locked from within
forbidding entry to all passwords.
Here instead of the roaring of a drunken street wanderer
the night wind brings moaning.
Here despite the silence of the sea and sky
the city is full of noises, void of words.

In absence of the moon, I have stepped drunkenly on this alien beach
but have kept sober.
I am happy that like the minaret of the sea
I have vigilantly clutched the red lantern of my heart in my hands

all through the night. (*Earth and Time*, June 1991)

NATURE AND NATURALISM

Naderpour is a poet of nature in all aspects. He is able to feel into two young sparrows in search of water. "Thirst" reminds the reader of Keats's "Ode to A Nightingale" or of Shelly's "Ode to a Skylark." Here the power of joining with two sparrows reflects the typical romantic negative capability of which Keats spoke:

Thirst

A happy day in late March;
after clouds wept
in the heart of the desert
the smiling sun
had spread golden dust
on tree branches.

Spring's wet wind
carried the smell
of the thirsty desert.
Tree branches, like strong dark arms,
mingled in light with the rain's ointment.
More agile than the breeze, two young sparrows
flew from the nest;
ignorant of their first spring's grace
coming from a long voyage,
the world and spring became young in their eyes.

They perched on a tree branch
and the sun dripped on their wings.
The blood of spring ran passionately
in the capillaries of leaves
upon which they stood.
The pulse of the young feverish branch
drummed feverishly.
An offshoot suddenly ripened and burst out

of the skin under their tender feet,
an abscess on the tree's arm.
Like a sleeper displaced by an earthquake,
the little sparrows flew away,
separating from one another in fear
while spreading their shadow.
First love grew in their hearts.

A burning fever overcame them,
making them thirsty.
In vain, they looked for a drop of water,
as the clouds had finished weeping,
and the sun had drank the earth.
On the protuberance of an old branch
a glittering drop.
The beaks motioned in joy
flying to catch it,
but just before wetting their mouths
it fell on the ground,
snatched like a pearl
as they reached for it
by the sun's crystal hand!

In the feverish noondays of spring,
when the sun splashes dust over wet branches,
the little sparrows who know spring's kindness
in the ardor of their thirst
fly over their nest, searching everywhere,
but always coming back home, every night
thirstier than before! (*The Grapes Poem*, May 21, 1957)

The memory of Keats is revived in another poem of his, "Autumn." In this poem and Keats's "To Autumn," images abound and the poets use personifications of abstract concepts. However, a remarkable difference between the two is the outlook toward autumn. In Keats the reader beholds a very happy season. Even the last stanza that indicates the last month of the season, the end of the day and the end of life is expressed with a sense of hope: "Where are the songs of Spring? Ay, where are they? / Think not of them, thou hast thy music too." Naderpour becomes much more modern, the image is not happy at all. Autumn heralds loneliness, massacre of leaves, and putrefaction.

Autumn

1

The earth was scratching
its pocked body
with nails of water.
I looked up
into incessant rain.

As night was hiding
its fleeting attempts
to seize the moment,
I saw migrating pigeons
through vine branches.

From the downy limits of air
still wet from their feathers
relentless raindrops fall to the ground
like the eyes of pigeons.

2

Autumn's breeze at noon
fluffing like birds' wings
as the air released crow's songs over the city.

Under the copper clouds
the tired sun was going to bed,
the horizon like the enamel of earthenware
in its gunmetal light.

Black umbrellas unfolded in the streets
like thousands of black mushrooms.

3

The evening strewed the dust of calamity,
branches struck with death's fever,
dead bodies of leaves falling
under every footstep of rain.

The horizon on that cloudy night
colored an incandescent iron.
Stars: extinguished.
Windows: illuminated.

I looked at the alley:
no shoes but mine
scrubbing the ground.

Breeze, that wandering gypsy,
was moaning woefully
beside the corpse of every leaf. (*The Grapes Poem*, Tehran, 28 November, 1957)

There are reasons for the differences of attitude toward nature between Naderpour and a romantic like Keats. One outstanding one is in the time of the composition of some of such nature poems. Before the 1953 coup in Iran, there was a sense of the poet endowed with a sense of the mission and responsibility. After the coup, however, there was a shattering of the dream, and they took refuge in the world of imagination and seclusion.[3] The poet in this atmosphere is a modern Iranian: introvert, sullen, defeated, and dissident. Naderpour was no exception. "Thirst," "Autumn," "A Man Waiting for Himself," "Palmist," "Fortune" are a few examples in which nature like the poet withers and brings no hope. In the last two of aforementioned poems the speakers take to fatalism and naturalism in the sense that they feel they are victims of powers over which they have no control:

Palmist

The sun's hive had fallen over,
spilling bees full of light
on the sky's trodden grass
where twilight's crimson petals had grown.

Wind, the old palm-reader, appeared from a long distance,
an autumn yellow shawl around his neck,
coming to visit trees in the alley
to tell their fortunes clearly.

As every tree greeted him with every step he took
and every branch stretched towards him,
he brushed them aside
and like a gypsy sang a strange melody.

He sang on and on, so that the evening's crows
called for the night from among the trees.
Fearing that call, the leaves fell down
as if a thousand swallows were shot in the air.

Night flowed on the leaves like water,
each leaf like a cut palm.
The palmist wind had already foreseen their fortune
without reading any of them!(*The Sun's Kohl,* September 30, 1959)

Fortune

You star-crossed man!
Look at your dry and bare hands:
This is a lost and rudderless desert;
its earthly womb is devoid of any sprout.
A hair in this desert stands for a male blade of grass.
A drop of sweat fails to herald any spring.
And this intertwining serpent that poured nothing but sorrow's poison
becomes, alas, the itinerary of your life.
A pity for you,

you star-crossed man!
Look at the dark night of your fortune:
Once the spring of your heart brought forth no blossoms.
May the eve of your life be starless!
You star-crossed man!
A Pity for you! (*The Sun's Kohl*, Tehran, May 23, 1958)

Man and Nature

Nature to Naderpour is endowed with extreme power. He does not simply praise it, he is empathically united with it in such a way that what lies outside nature reflects his own human nature, emotions and thoughts. The boundaries between nature and self are lifted in other poems. In "Not Plant and Stone but Fire" the speaker is one with nature:

Not Plant or Stone, but Fire

I am born from the pure seed of the sun
in the dry lonely desert,
my splendor rooted in salty soil.

I am born from the inertia of stone,
the effort of wind, the speed of fire,
and the patience of water.
Under the evening's golden dome,
I stretch my arms toward the sky;
In the desert's glorious night
I am the last walking passenger.

The root of me, this old tree,
the desert's wise elder,
remains full with the free essence
of living, half-living, and dead plants.
The root of me, this old tree,
this valiant recluse
remains full with youthful sprouts,
fresh songs,
rivers' sediments,

and the sky's transparency.
My fresh fruits: small birds;
my dew drops: bright stars.
These birds of day,
these stars of night
having emerged from the opening of my broad chest
heralded love,
newer songs,
more pleasant intimations.

The wind like a mother plucking a few grey hairs
from her daughter's head
has shaken the yellow from my green leaves.
The sky above my branches,
softer than a dove's chest,
has spread blue velvet.
Harder than a heavy rock
through the whirlwind of years,
I remain with outstretched arms
rooted to the blazing fire.

Years have passed and my eyes
remain open towards the sky
with the promise of a great miracle:
the return of a man
who once passed my way. (*Not Plant*, Tehran, December 22, 1963)

A similar image is in the following poem from the same book of poems *Not plant and Stone, But Fire*. The poet turns the speaker into a tree and thus a man joins nature while nature through personification of natural images turns into humanity. Naderpour shows his power as a master of defamiliarization by his new outlooks.

A Man Waiting for Himself

Sparrow fruits grew on branches
and twilight poured the blood of light into rainwater.
An outlandish breeze blew from distant lands

carrying the scent of hope to the familiar soil.

Pawing the sky, the sun
scratched his bloody fingertips on the earth
as the irate Evening kept cursing in the ears of trees.
My heart, fearing the Night, moaned like a cat caught in a pit.
The flock of ravens belonged to the body of the night,
the horizon in the trees was like a carpet's pattern.
That night I was just returning from a date
like an old frame devoid of my own picture.

I heard a sound behind me in the silence of the woods,
turning around, I found myself behind me.
My eyes popped out of their sockets.
I feared I'd gone blind.

Like a bird from a branch my head flew from my neck,
a dry vessel growing in its place.
My emaciated body, like the bones of the dead,
was enough for the breeze, the sniffing dog.

Beside the forest road flowing like a stream
all of a sudden, I became a tree, unable to move.
I turned back to see a mass of trees,
like weary wanderers, lining up behind me.
I found myself in a thin column of light
fading and hiding in the dark woods.
I told my heart that I could catch up with it if I ran
but can a tree turn back into a man?

My glance passed through the leaves and came back in dismay.
The branches of my waiting were fertilized.
I kept waiting for myself,
hoping that he might pass by.

Now it is evening and the sky
bloody in the horizon from among trees like a carpet pattern.

I am lonely in the dense woods,

an old frame devoid of my own picture.

Sparrow fruits grow on branches,
the earth has washed away the blood of light with rainwater,
I am all ears to the whisper of wind passing by,
perhaps hoping to hear some familiar news.... (*Not Plant*, Tehran, December 10, 1960)

It does not matter whether the speaker is one with a tree as in "A Man Waiting for Himself," feels one with a tree as in "A Mutual Secret," or addresses a tree as in "No Blossom, No Bird." There is no hope for a future spring since the poet perceives the spring is of life is gradually going:

A Mutual Secret

Shhh...A secret in the silence of the breeze,
the tree unable to express a need beyond
recurring youth from the spring,
as if shut against the cool air.

Or else a wordless request,
an apprehensive hope,
a pause of longing to fly
closer to the sun.

"Which is it then?" I ask
in my attempt to translate nature.
One moves, the other stands,
a strained relation.

I share the tree's pain,
its yellow, its green.
Like the tree I wish to fly
closer to the sun.

Because the tree remains mute under leaves,
I scream for it, with its own red tongue:
"You heartless breeze, take us toward spring

to know the eternal sun!" (*The Last Supper*, Tehran, July 1, 1971)

No Blossom, No Bird

Poor tree!
Have the heavens and the earth left you
waiting for spring?

Don't you know your leaves,
like birds, have flown away
one by one?
The sun, this yellow spider,
will no longer weave its web of golden days
among your leaves.

The jeweled ring of the moon
will no longer twinkle
on your branch fingers.

The small sparrows' nest
will no longer beat, like a heart,
in your green clothes.

Their nest was your heart;
a symbol of your nakedness.
Any wonder why it no longer beats?

Your leaves, like birds,
charred in the autumn fire
have fallen at your foot,
and homeless sparrows
gone to the wilderness
with the wind and the leaves.

But now, poor tree!
You stand on your own unmarked grave
like a bone-rotted corpse.
Look! You've lost all you had.
Sit down; no blossom will smile any longer,
and there is no room for laughter.

Sit down; from now on
no bird will fly over a nest;
no bird appears in this metallic sky.

Poor tree!
Have the heavens and the earth left you
waiting for spring? (*Not Plant,* Tehran, July 31, 1960)

Pessimism reaches the climax in "Cigarettes." The abject poet-speaker sees his days burning down to a dismal end like smoked cigarettes:

Cigarettes

Every day at noon,
I ride my legs home
like the wind through alleyways.

Under my feet,
half-smoked, stamped upon cigarettes
sleep with smoke and dust.

Every evening,
the sun's broken cart takes me through alleyways of life
to death's abode.

Under the wheels of the sun's cart
these half-burnt, trampled upon days
sleep with smoke and dust. (*Not Plant,* Tehran, August 10, 1960)

WOMAN AND NATURE

Naderpour has a complex attitude towards women in his long poetical career. All in all, he regards women as powerful and a source of inspiration. At times, they become soul mates, inspiring the speaker with romantic feelings. At other times, the female becomes an erotic and sexual object, and in many occasions she is an inseparable part of nature. Being a pictorial poet by nature, Naderpour presents fine natural designs with a feminine backdrop. In the following poem, "Eye and Hands," the night engulfs the speaker in the form of a human body. There is no direct reference to a woman, but the way eyes and hands are described suggests their feminine nature. The timing of the composition of the poem in Paris has an implication of the influence of the poet by European currents in romantic poetry.

Eyes and Hands

The night came. Terror behind its hidden gaze
struck me with the shudder of death.
From my deepest memories
an animal I seemed to know groped around
and caught me.

In its wild hands, I lay still,
too afraid to call for help.
A star winked overhead, as if taking aim,
and moonlight struck my eye like an arrow.

One moment, the sky, trees, and clouds
came together, then faded away.
One moment sinful eyes
appeared from behind dark curtains.

Like a mood ring, changing color with rage,
the earth had filled with dust and darkness.
One moment everything turned dead silent.
The fear of annihilation overcame the world.

Out of nowhere a pair of blazing eyes
began to grow towards me.
Two tiny red seeds
blossomed into fire.

As time dripped like a tear from the eye of death itself
and all of life withered from its momentary drips,
in the light of those quivering eyes

two wild paws crushed my throat.

Under its cold fingers I lay still,
too afraid to call for help.
A star winked overhead, as if taking aim,
and moonlight struck my eye like an arrow.

I moaned through the darkness
but nobody heard me
in the panting breeze.
My voice died in my throat. (*Eyes and Hands*, Paris, March 15, 1952)

In the following poem it is difficult to ascertain whether a tree is described in terms of a woman or vice versa. The title suggests it is a tree but in the poem one sees the woman in terms of a tree.

A Lover Looks at a Tree

Your body's aroma,
Your lovely tall figure,
Your warm blood,
Your blossoming breasts,
Your gracefully long legs,
awaken spring in me.

In the curve around your hips,
In your short dress,
an eye or a mouth,
or, even kinder, a heart,
a small hidden nest,
home to birth and rising,
full of the sun's warm,
restating the story of infatuation.

I am in love with your grace
and would suffer your pains. (*From the Sublime*, Tehran, June 6, 1970)

"A Heart Shaped Stone" and "A Natural Map," however, clearly describe a woman not as a tree but many elements in nature contribute in her production. The limbs and the human attributes have counterparts in nature such as days, water, the approach of morning, the spring, fate and fortune, stars, the sun, and last but not least the stone as the heart.

A Heart Shaped Stone

Your long legs:
a picture of crystalline days
when I descended from heights
to wash my burnt feet
in the bright water
of childhood's spring.

Your footsteps bring morning
with the new year's silvery shoes
in spring alleyways.

Your hands reach with the Caretaker
toward the cradle of my life
to swing me in joy through the world.

Your eyes, stars in a nest,
bring good news of the future;
reflecting the smile of Fate.

Shine on me.
Rise in me.
Turn me into a mirror,
into running water,
till your crystalline hand
comes through your sleeve,
searching my chest for a piece
of heart-shaped stone. (*The Last Supper*, Tehran, January, 1974.)

Natural Map

She belonged to the earth's naked body:

soft white soil
with two burning hills
embraced by the sun
and two arms of a river
flowing down
to a shameful cleft
at the bottom of which
grew a wet patch of grass
watered by a spring
as red as a smile.

I wept in the evening
of her narrow ravine. (*The Last Supper*, Tehran, October, 1975)

In a very similar trend to the above poems, "My Poem as Flagon of Wine" describes a woman in terms of nature. However, for the first time the poet describes the beloved as his own poem.

My Poem as a Flagon of Wine

You are like a flagon of wine:
the crystal spiral
(a gift of the glass blower),
runs down your delicate frame
like a curl of hair.
You are like a flagon of wine:
in the glitter of morning
the slope of your chest
to your narrow neck
fills with drunken light.
You are like a flagon of wine, my poem.

How can I, at times, avoid thinking of your fragility?
If you break, you'll spill my thirst.
A friend of mirrors,
you speak the language of flowers.
How blissful your rising between light and the world,

the sun in horizons of spring grass.

Your lips: the mouth of the rose at dawn.
A breeze of a word will open them,
the flower's tongue on the wind.

Tall crystal,
turn me into wine and pour me in your throat.
Let me into your transparent chest.
Grant me the heat of a greenhouse in winter.
Drink me all over,
or else give the last drop to the drunk.
You are like a flagon of wine.
How quickly you shatter. (*False Dawn*, Tehran, September 6, 1977)

NATURE: MORNING, EVENING

Nature in Naderpour is a complex concept. He does not have one constant attitude towards it. He sometimes approaches it for its sheer beauties, for its imagistic defamiliarization, sympathizing with it in a romantic mode, finding in it human attributes of love, life, and death. Sometimes he is pessimistic about nature when he ponders the passage of life or when he is in exile or in 1950s when the coup brought about a pessimistic atmosphere among intellectuals in Iran. In "Autumn" everything is gloomy but with a nostalgic flashback to childhood memories; about three decades later, he has a totally different view of autumn and winter when he remembers "red and yellow sycamore leaves,/ Like colorful panes of the public bath of the village" in whose cold winter when he becomes "an adventurous knight" facing "the light of future" ("A Future in the Past"). He sees heroism in nature when he is patriotic, but eroticism in it when he is in love. Depending on the times and mood of the poet, we see different pictures of nature. Poems about morning are naturally different from those addressing evening; the same is true with different seasons. In the following poem, composed at Christmas, depicts a winter morning:

The Holy Spirit

The spirit of the morning
hangs fruit on the virgin tree;
from its green womb
a bird is born, and flies
toward the red opening
in the sun.

A brother to light,
this happy bird. (*From the Sublime*, Tehran, December, 1969)

In another epigrammatic poem, morning, spring, a bird and the poet unite:

Morning 1

In the shy blue sky,
a bird, in search of morning,
whistled, "Where?"
"On your wings," I replied.

The bird flew away,
and I saw morning
in the blinking of my eyes. (*The Last Supper*, Tehran, April 26, 1971)

In the following two poems the speaker becomes one with the sun:

From Me to the Sun

The dusk surged
and the wind's wild hand
clashed the windows like two cymbals.
I looked at the trees
through their bare chest bones;
the sun, big and bloody, kept pounding, kept beating;
The beats, in tiny dust particles
and through red blood vessels of copper wires,
reverberated like African drums
in my breath, my own rhythms, and my temple.

I saw a mysterious connection between the sun,
this big fiery heart of the trees,
and the small warm heart of mine.
A connection between my heartbeats and tiny dust particles,
between wires, railways of sound and light, and the tic-tock of
the wall clock,
I saw I was not separate from the sun
and from water, and the tree and the earth.
Behind the window a man passed.
His legs had started a voyage
with my heart and its beats;
he breathed in my heart
he took steps with my heartbeats,
but his heart
in company with the sun's heart
kept beating and pounding in the bare bones of the trees.

The evening spread forth its shadows.
My look returned from the long line of the trees
towards its reflection
and the sound of my heart
burst the mirror. (*Not Plant*, Tehran, May 21, 1964)
From Dot to Circle

I looked at the sun for moments
then closed my eyes,
Under my lids
a dot
turned round and round and round
and made a circle.
Like a stone skipping on water
a dot
turned round and round and round
till it became a circle.

I opened eyes and became the sun. (*Not Plant*, Tehran, Summer, 1964)

Nature

The Capsized Sun

Like a woman closing windows
one by one
and turning off the light,
night extinguished the stars
and went to bed.
The red in the white sky of dawn
painted crimson flowers
on the milk-white waterfall.
Some wind expounded
upon the green book of trees.
Then fire flourished in the silky grass.
Not a real fire
on the green sea,
but a boat,
a telling capsized sun
or, the explosion of a dark swelling
In anemone's red sun. (*The Last Supper,* Tehran, July 10, 1971)

The poet not only finds the sun's curve above the sea as a capsized boat but also sees it in the form of anemone. In the original, the poet plays on the Persian words *qâyeq* 'boat,' *haqâyeq*, 'truth,' and *shaqâyeq* 'anemone,' another ample evidence of his power of imagination both in the realm of lexicon and imagery.

It seems there is no end in Naderpour's imaginative novelty to seeing old concepts in new dress. In "Prayer at Sunrise," the sun is seen as a red-skinned Indian in terms of color and feathered headdress as sun rays. As the poem is in the form of a prayer, the speaker is hopeful of a sunrise and a resurrection with its mythic overtones:

Prayer at Sunrise

Red-skinned Indian,
how do you feel on a polar night?
Has the chilling silence

driven you to sleep?
Or has oblivion blotted out
the cold reality of past white days?

Can't you recall
those August afternoons
when a violet cackle
beamed from your mouth,
the gold fire of your breath
burning heaven and earth?

What hand splashed your blood
against the iceberg
on a polar night,
leaving you dormant
in the prison cell
of your enemies?

Red skinned Indian,
you need no allotted day
of resurrection.
With this call to prayer
awake in feathered headdress.
Arise, O sun, once more! (*The Last Supper*, Tehran, December 6, 1974)

In "Smoke after Burning," there is a radical shift of attitude toward the sun. The inclusion of the poem in *False Dawn* makes it clear that the poet is dismayed at a true sunrise. There are reasons for this change. On a personal level, this poem and "From the Depths" are the poet's reflection of the passage of life and the appearance of white hair on the head and a constant reminder that old happy days of youth, "that distant morning," are over. On an impersonal level, the timing of the composition of the poem coincides with political and social turmoil in Iran, about a year before the revolution about which Naderpour was so cynical. The reference to "message of prophets" and "the museum of [his] imagination" might indicate the poet's yearning for a rebirth of some old glory to which he has been waiting in vain. The sun will now reveal ruins and the depth of the damage:

>Smoke after Burning
>
>You gloomy bright rising!
>Are you the morning of puberty,
>that distant morning whose golden lights
>beamed through the museum of my imagination
>to display trunks and faces,
>to animate and move blood through the statues of my mind?
>
>That distant morning in whose light
>I put lips on the forehead of mirrors
>and my kisses nestled in breath's vapor
>and that alien twin, from the other side of my image
>with a response, acquaints my lips?
>
>That distant morning that in my eyes
>changed a leaf into a hand
>and then a hand into a tongue with magical powers
>and then, on the leaf tongue, made the message of the breeze
>more fluent than the messages of prophets?
>
>You gloomy bright rising!
>You distant morning that has risen again!
>Now from the hatching of my eyes
>you are shining on a burnt museum
>on a museum whose statues are molten
>and smoke after fire has still lingers;
>now you are left with a vacant mirror
>whose falling mercury
>has opened old eyes on the night of blindness
>and has removed the imprint of my twin's lips and my kisses
>faster than the vapor of breaths
>
>Now you shine on fallen leaves
>with foreign tongues with the breeze and the birds.
>Leaves like hands buried in mud.

Is it a problem if these hands shake with compassion?

You gloomy bright sun!
Ruins are still thirsty for your light.
Close the doors to the terminable night!
After such a rise, may your dusk be unlawful!
If there remains no morning,
tell the night too to die. (*False Dawn,* Tehran, November 29, 1977)

In the following poem, the reference to youth is more highlighted:

From the Depths

Morning upon the horizon,
I dove from shallow waters
to the deep reaches of time,
looking for the eternal pearl of youth
to present to humans
to stop the sun casting his evil eye upon them,
to make the mirror show only young faces.
The night came with his dark blue stars.
The sea dragged me down into his wide mouth.
I joined mermaids

In senility I learned
the secrets of water's eternal youth
and grew younger.
Lulled into sleep by the depths,
I remained heedless of morning on the mountain,
and of night in the galaxy.

Morning upon the horizon,
I dove from shallow waters
to the deep reaches of time,
hunting fragile female figures....

Bright lamp of the shore, call me! (*False Dawn,* Tehran, June 9, 1978)

It is not unexpected from a poet preoccupied with nature to be interested in all aspects of nature. Evening and night are still more dominant images in Naderpour. However, he deals with them in his own way: personification and defamiliarization. In the pithy poem, "Evening," the atmosphere of a cesarean delivery is created for a natural phenomenon:

Evening

Wind's sharp sword
severed water's protruding belly.
From the incision, the sun's blood-stained fish
was thrown on the beach
like a warm heart.
The old sea foamed and moaned.
The night heard the moan
and settled beside her bed. (*The Sun's Kohl*, Tehran, August 8, 1959)

In "Before Sunset," the touch of sunlight on wet ground is described in terms of a man washing scorched feet in rainwater:

Before Sunset

After rain,
the sun washes his scalded feet
in still waters.
Under his boots,
autumn extinguishes leaves
like red flames.

In the small room,
at the rear of the garden,
behind the firelight,
her long naked leg.... (*The Last Supper*, Tehran, July 5, 1971)

As the night approaches, new images of darkness appear. In a terse poem, "Tooth and Diamond," the stars and crickets are described as diamonds breaking:

> Tooth and Diamond
>
> Behind thick dark lips
> night smashed the diamond of each star
> against its teeth
> with one blow
> and from each crunch
> thousands of crickets screeching. (*Time and Earth*, April 25, 1987)

NATURE AND DEATH

The night has an association with death. However, Naderpour is able to see the image of death not only in time but in other natural images. There are four consecutive poems, composed within a month or so in Paris, which address death in different ways. The first one is death of a tree, the second one of a butterfly, the third a hunted hunter, and the fourth imaginary "dawn's cockscombs":

> 1. Talking Tree
>
> This year in the silence of autumn
> no woodcutter's song,
> no sign of his dark shadow,
> no road trembling under his feet.
> My praying arms stretch toward spring.
> My legs get stuck up to the knee in mud.
> On my head the mass of migrating clouds;
> On my heart the sizzle of the sun;
> On my back the knife's old graffiti;
> And in my rib cage, a bird calls nightly,
> "Where is the axe?" (*From the Sublime*, Paris, December, 1966)

2. Under the Shadow of Two Blue Finger

In the morning light
it perched on a flower
with multi-colored wings,
sinking its head
into an imaginary spring
reflected in the dew.

The antenna motioned
at the alien light
feeling the weight of the sunbeam
on the scale of its two wings.
As it pretended to sleep,
the wind rocked it to sleep.

And in its slumber
it saw the flight
of a light-speckled shadow
around its cradle of petals
attempting to fly away.
The shadow crumbled.

With colorful wings
it landed
on paper,
no longer with the weight
of a sunbeam
upon its flight.
Under the blue shadow
of two fingers
a pin pierced the head
of the butterfly. (*From the Sublime,* Paris, December, 1966)

3. Hunting

This is a hunting day.
I set out to the mountain's edge
where the dense forest frowns

under the sun's broad smile.
When the bullet zips, I vanish.
The lioness leaps like the spark
from a struck stone,
sinking her fangs in my throat,
coloring my shirt with fresh blood
that splashes to the ground like yoke.
My brain gushes under the wet vines. (*From the Sublime*, Paris, December, 1966)

4. Resurrection

They have cut off the dawn's cockscomb
and buried it.
Dense clusters of tulips rise from the ground.
Listen, Wind!
These bloody tulips cry:
"Are you awake, Dawn?
Do you wish to see us, Dawn?" (*From the Sublime*, Paris, January, 1967)

NATURE AND POLITICS

Since 1979, the 10-day period between the return of Ayatollah Khomeini from exile to the country and the victory of the revolution has been named "the 10-Days of Dawn (of the Islamic Revolution)." The poems in *False Dawn* composed in the period between 1977 and 1981 thus acquire more symbolic overtones as the poet fuses notions of disillusionment with the return of youth and what he sees as the bleak prospects of the revolution. The main noticeable point is that after the Islamic revolution for a short period there is a high frequency of religious terms such as mosque, minarets, prayer call, unity, and so on. The poems have temporarily socio-political overtones.

In the 1982 introduction to *False Dawn* published in Paris, Naderpour explicitly shows his concern about the future of the country with the Islamic revolution. He calls his clairvoyance "a sober sense," which like the protesting mass with clenched fists, believed that the evil should have been done away with but unlike the madding crowd it did not propose the elimination of the lesser evil by a greater one. He voiced his fear that the deceived people were, despite their good will, blindly obeying a reactionary and darkling idealism, and idealism for which great figures in Persian literature like Firdausi, Khayyam, Hafiz, Dehkhoda, Irajmirza, and Hedayat had fought. For such reasons, he could not see a happy ending to that movement. He said that the same feeling in him, in the evening of day of the victory of the uprising, put this question in a poem, "A Night by Himself," whether blood-hued color of the dawn was "the fag end of heresy or an asset of religion."

Naderpour maintains that the true history of a nation should be sought in its literature and that the art of poetry is a revelation in the unknown and a poem is a ray of light into darkness. If so, then many poems in *False Dawn* are both history and revelation, both truth and prophecy though none chant a motto or chronicle anything since poetry has nothing to do with such "commitments." At the end Naderpour dedicates the collection first to those sober ones who had divined the danger much in advance and then to those who compensate their yesterday's ignorance with today's insight and have decided on a manly battle with the enemies of Iran.

Naderpour's poetical life is paradoxical. He is political especially in the later years but not a political poet nor meant to be one. The views he voiced after the revolution in newspapers outside Iran are sharp, but when he comes to poetry he treats it as if it were too dear, too sacred to taint it with the unholy. Even when he was political in rare cases, literary aspects of his poems outweighed the political dimensions. He was a believer in the nature of poetry to express indirectly, figuratively. A few poems that bear on the revolution are all symbolic and he, as it is his wont, borrows images from nature.

The first poem of this series is "A Doubt in Storm" composed at the time of volatile demonstrations against the Shah and a few months before his deposition. The poet compares the multitude of people as a madding crowd who have no ears for the truth expressed by the poet-prophet, a truth expressing bird whose throat is cut by a lightning:

A Doubt in Storm

The red lash of lightning on the sky's back
left a question mark.
The sky screamed an answer.

The lash trickled from the torn sky onto my brain,
the blood of raindrops
like an army of big, cold ants
marching down my head and camping on my chest.
Bubbles blistered the water's face;
black mushroom spikes sprouted from the earth
as the moon slowly rotted
the banks of the bog
in violent wind.

A strange dream grew through my body,
circling like blood,
filling my certainties with doubt.

I ran outside myself: a branch from a tree.
I sank into myself: a stagnant lagoon.
(My heart divided between growth and decay).

In my ears: the breeze a fly's moan
for the propagation of filth.
In my eyes: the crescent an inverted horseshoe[4]
for the ignoble fortune and fame.

I found a way through the bog and the jungle.
Standing still, I asked myself,
"Which one?
Should I put the bog before or behind?
Or should I remove the young jungle before my eyes
And plant it behind my back?"

The jungle: full of uprising incensed trees,
individual babbles.[5]
an inarticulate orator
versus a prophet with an alien oracle.

The bog: dormant mind of horizons,
ignorant mirror-handler[6] of the rising sun.
The bog: fish cemetery,
scroll of the night's passing and the moon's passing away.[7]

Uncertain between jungle and the bog
I stood still on my two feet,
"Which one?
Should I put the bog before or behind?
Or should I remove the young jungle before my eyes
And plant it behind my back?"

The red lash of lightning on the sky's back
left a question mark,
drawing a clear sketch of my secret inquiry.
The moaning of a mourning dove lost amid thunder's rage,
the blood of his cut throat spilled on the ground.
I told myself:
"In the storm of fury and blood
what melody can come
from the larynx of a screech owl?"[8] (False Dawn, Tehran, 5 September, 1978)

"A Midnight Sun" was likewise composed amid the political unrests about a couple of months before the victory of the revolution. It is the poet's horrible apocalyptic vision of the future that he assumed would remain one relegated to by-gone ages. The dominant imagery comes from an allusion to the story of Moses who saw a fire at night and that was the start of his prophethood. There are further clues to his story like a word play on the Persian word *shabân,* meaning 'at night' and 'shepherd,' as well as alluding to a yarmulke. The light and darkness imagery in a religious setting with a man dressed in "a gown belonging to ancient slaves" who talked about a "miracle" during turbulent days in Iran entices one to associate the poem with the events in Iran those days.

Again, the poet never succumbs into direct reaction to the events but has his own poetic take on them. He is skeptical of the turn of the events, so he calls that sun a "false sun." The plural "we" as opposed to "the man" is a clear indication that a religious man is addressing a crowd who imagines that they see the sun. Naderpour might be saying that religions have not brought about 'enlightenment' and this holds true for the 1979 revolution. Naderpour is disagreeing with the idea that religions have played a role as sources of enlightenment to humanity.

A still more cogent interpretation is Naderpour's dismay with the return of the power and the flame of youth which obsessed his mind all the time. This is an age-old concept which reminds us of Shakespeare's "in me thou seest the twilight of such day" and "the glowing of such fire/ that on the ashes of his youth doth lie." The poem is also a reminder of W. B. Yeats's "A Second Coming" in which "things fall apart" and hope turns into dismay. In the latter "Surely some revelation is at hand" as in the former "that miracle is at hand."

Both poems rely heavily on light and darkness imagery as well. One was written in 1919 in the aftermath of the first World War and the other in the heat of a revolution:

A Midnight Sun

1

The man was saying, "The sun will shine at that corner"
(pointing to a spot).
We looked that way.
A red spot was burning at the furthest corner of the dim night;
the man was saying, "The sun is no longer that old desert wanderer
who every day sewed east and west together,
but a straight-backed, slim-waisted,

dark haired and golden-eyed young man
clad in silk as delicate as light,
a coronet on his head like the crest of hoopoes,
boots redder than ducks' webbed feet
riding a horse and would not stop
to invite you watch the world.

We all imagined the young sun;
it made us weep.

2

Although we saw that the night was entirely black
the man was saying, "The miracle is at hand."
We looked at where he pointed to once more;
suddenly lightning in that promised spot sparked a conflagration;
a corner of the dark night burned away in that bloody fire.
An old man emerged from the flames:
his hair strewed like hay
from under a cap shaped like a yarmulke
in a gown belonging to ancient slaves;
his fat body, short,
his flaming red eyes, tearful,
his lame legs like the old desert wanderer, bare;
his burnt paws went bleeding.
In horizon, for a moment, he stood like the first morning,
afterwards turning back to leave.
We all saw the false sun at midnight;
we wept so hard that we burst into laughter.... (*False Dawn*, Tehran, November 30, 1978)

"A Night by Himself" was written on the same day that the Shah's regime collapsed. The dominant imagery is that of the *False Dawn* in which the poem appears: light and darkness. Added to that is a motif of blindness and insight. The speaker repeatedly calls people blind and sees himself in his drunkenness "the most keen-sighted man" and "the wisest fool." With Tiresian clairvoyance, he warns against the future but finds no ear as "the loneliest man." The greatest clue to help a keen reader discern that the poem is a symbolic take on the events is the date of the composition. In fact, in this particular case, with a reference, one could easily read too much into the poem.

A Night by Himself

When in darkness
lights in distant houses
flutter more than newborn bees
building nests in branches,
and when the moon mounts the tree-saddles
to ride through evening alleyways
behind this thin curtain,
I am the loneliest man
in a house more silent than the solitude of specters,
more sorrowful than the song of drunks wandering through the night.
You gods of solitude!
You gods!
Consider me an associate of horror, a roommate of pain.

This thin curtain
through which the wintery moonlight
infiltrates my room
is a magic mirror:
the red coals of the fireplace
glow as if the picture of rising sun
lies upon it.
This new dawn on the horizon
colors my individual thoughts
with the full spectrum of light.
Days give birth and die,
some with smiling lips, others with weeping eyes.
These endless phantasms
keep me both drunk and sober,
cold and warm.
With an open heart and a blind man's gaze
I have a dreadful dream

that my words dare not express,
though when I open my mouth
I become the most articulate man.

Yes, in this horrible dream
I reclaim the crimson dawn of birth.
In the crimson dusk of old age
I ask myself which one is it:
colorful anemones of happiness
in the land of childhood
or the wistful tulips of old age
on the eve of being trampled?
I must be drunk to find these two compatible.
I'd have never thought this sober dream
the antidote of drunkenness.
You gods of sagacity!
You gods!
I am so drunk that in the eyes of the wise
I become the most infamous man.
Beyond this thin curtain
I find the evening filled with moonlight.
The blood that laughs at the alley tree
tells me, "Sir, this crimson is not the one you imagined,
change your mind about it."

If at the dawn of youth you found the dried blood of birds
after the arrival of a guest
to prepare a chicken for a welcome feast,[9]
on the eve of old age
you will find the spurting blood of the young on earth
before the onslaught of the enemies.
If on the earthen rooftops of childhood, you could trace the arrows of angels
piercing through the chest of the Satan at night,[10]
now you can find thousands of bullets in innocent chests.
Sir, these nights are different. Sir, those nights have passed.
Think twice about it!
On this night of drunkenness, I return, silent and furious.
From the report of red blood to sobriety,

> I tell myself there is no insight in the drunkard.
> But I am content that in this dark land
> I am the most keen-sighted man.
> The big city, like a vast basin, remains asleep.
> My eyes see, beyond the moonlit curtain,
> floating fish of lights
> twinkling green, silver, and golden.
> The horizons are colored by dusk.
> I ask myself,
> Is this the red of morning or evening?
> Is this flaming blood
> the match end of heresy or an spark of religion?
> I will not wait for an answer.
> With all my folly,
> consider me the wisest man,
> the wisest fool.... (False Dawn, Tehran, February 11, 1979)

Almost a year later, still in Tehran, he insists on calling the revolution a false dawn. Nature pathetically cries but no hope for a real dawn:

False Dawn

> Tonight the earth has said farewell to all his sins.
> Snow's white piety has covered up all heresies of the earth.
> This sliver mask
> on the black face of nature
> is the world's most beautiful lie.
> Tonight the old tree
> imagines that he is young
> but after the sun's nativity
> his snowy thoughts will melt.
> What eyes
> like the sun
> can behold the hidden face of truth?
> Perhaps eyes after tears
> can reply to this question.
>
> You old tree!
> What kind of cry is the rain?

It is as vast as the sorrow of heaven
on the earth's oblivion.
A cry that darkens the snow's false dawn
in the short-lived evening of your adolescence
but takes you closer to the distant light of childhood,
a cry that can bestow on the eyes of the old
a translucent sight
as the childlike eye of the sun.

You rooster waiting for morning,
the fire will not die in cotton.
But look:
the sun is dead in white horizons,
the charming snow has closed
the eyes of ordinary trees,
and embarked with these walking patient villagers
at old age
on an imaginary vehicle
to the illusory city of adolescence.
But the earth's heart
yearns for the cry of the rain;
at night there lies the hidden truth.
You blacker than clouds of sorrow!
Bestow on me a never-ending cry.
You kind tear!
Bestow on my eyes the vision of a child! (*False Dawn*, Tehran,
23 January, 1980)

Seven years later, now living abroad, on the day of the anniversary of the revolution Naderpour writes "On the Eve of the Spring." There were many famous revolutionary songs reiterating that the winter, both literal and figurative were left behind and a new spring was ahead. The songs are ever since sung at anniversary of the revolution. The poet has both meanings of the spring in mind but with an ironic edge. A new nostalgic dimension is now added to Naderpour's poetry. The homesick speaker finds himself as a tree in winter. The last line is clear that the poem is about a homesick poet, but like "A Night by Himself," the date of the composition tells the reader how to interpret the poem. In a naturalistic mood he sees God's wrath responsible for his blight.

> On the Eve of the Spring
>
> On the eve of the spring, I am a tree in winter.
> Blossoms on my naked body grin sardonically.
> How can I know about the sweet smile of the dawn
> when, in the endless night, I have been a witness of rain's weeping?
> I will not see the green splendor of spring on this land.
> The ruins of my memory have yellowed in the fall.
> God's wrath shook my childhood home so hard
> that sleeping soil became my cradle.
> In this strange land, O heart, who should show me the way
> while, like a fallen leaf, I'm caught in the hands of the storm?
> I can see no difference between good and bad days.
> My days look like my nights, my spring like my winter.
> The heart beating in terror within my turbulent chest,
> does not wish to travel or risk adventure.
> I am a slave to the power of the sun:
> When he turns off his light,
> he will not mind my black prison of fear.
> Where is the breeze of dawn, after a pure rain,
> to invite me to the pleasant smell of the soil
> in your memory, Iran! (*Blood and Ashes*, February 11, 1987)

In "Trees and I" the only direct political reference is the poet's note on the title of the poem in which he writes, "On the extensive California wildfires in the fall of 1993 and in memory of the conflagration in Iran on February 11, 1979." That is the date of the victory of the revolution. The reader is immediately invited to take the poem as more or less symbolically, although in the poet's note a real fire is mentioned. Thus, Naderpour evades the temptation to write a merely political poem. The speaker sympathizes with California burning trees that are unable to flee the fire set up by Lucifer but suddenly identifies himself with a tree in that he is unable to move. The romantic love for and union with nature in Naderpour now takes a political hue.

Nature

Trees and I

The fire Lucifer kindled that night,
before sending a blaze into the sky,
spread through the city of angels,
once more capturing Eden
with the fire of his sin.

On a black night, with one touch of the pen
on the natural map of the earth,
he drew the climate of blood and wrath.

With the wind he sent forth thousands of sparks,
with soot-black snow falling
from the red sky
down to the dark earth.

The sparks from his night fire
gave birth to a race of stars, like phosphorous mosquitoes,
in a sea basin.

On that wonderful night
a big assembly of trees around me
burning with feet chained to the ground
were thinking of escape
from the fiery wind
frantically blowing
on their naked bodies
shivering to death.

In that green throng,
I remained unaware of my own burning among them.
Like all trees, and better than any human,
I could sense the pain of their staying as they longed to escape.

The fire of memory blazed inside me
through the scattered smoke of years,
the burning past before my eyes
witnessing the mad rising in the sky

above those sleeping, ignorant residents of the earth.

On that wonderful night
the trees pointed to their feet,
to show me that their problem
needed a solution.
But for me escape remained inescapable[11]
because I quickly saw
the enemy living in my house.
I left my home for a foreign land.

The night when the fiend's fuming breath
burnt the city of the earth's city of angels
and the hell in the dead of the night began shining
I found myself pinned to the ground inside the hidden fire of memory.
Unable to hear my own voice
I called, "You trees, relatives of the earth,[12]
with these agile legs of mine still unbound,
where do I have to take refuge
from this great fire?
I know no way but this one: a sudden flight with the night wind
like the smoke, over the fire, toward annihilation.
(Time and Earth, December 16, 1993)

Notes

1. In Persian, *tabût* 'coffin' and *barût* 'powder' rhyme.
2. A word-for-word translation is "the cross chest of the luminous crossroads." The lines refer to modern man's crucifixion.
3. See Hossein Shakki, "Taghazzol va Âsheqâneh-sarâ'i dar Âsâre Nâder Nâderpûr" ("Lyricism and Love Poetry in Nader Naderpour"). *Hafiz Monthly* 33 (August 2006): 73-78.
4. The Shia' clergy wear a certain kind of sandal *na'lain* meaning 'two shoes' in Arabic. In modern Persian *na'l* means 'horseshoe' which in Arabic it has the same meaning. The poet is making a pun bringing together the crescent moon, a symbol of Islam, horseshoes, and the shoes of the clergy and that they are making a good fortune in the name of religion.
5. Translator's note: Thinking about this expression, which is in fact a pleonasm, I talked to a colleague, an expert on Persian literature at Yasouj University. She asked me, "Who used this bizarre expression?" I thought it might have been because of rhyming constraints. So I used "rhetorical quibbles." However, based on the context and especially the following two lines, I think we should use a meaningless expression like 'verbal quibbles' to stress the meaninglessness of events.
6. The original is something that might be translated as a "mirror handler," a person who holds a mirror especially before the bride and bridegroom in weddings.
7. *Sargozasht*, 'narrative, story;' *dargozasht*, 'pass away.'
8. A reference to the poet. In Persian a scops owl is called *morghe haqq* 'the bird of truth,' a kind of onomatopoeia.
9. At one time, especially in rural regions, when a guest arrived, a chicken or a rooster was killed and cooked immediately as there were no refrigerators to preserve food. The blood after a guest suggests a happy occasion but in the poem it brings no joyous news.
10. In summer time it was usual to sleep on rooftops. The image comes from the passage of meteors in the sky and the way children would take them as arrows of angels.
11. A play on the words *goriz*, escape, and *gozir*, choice.
12. A word play on *bastegân* meaning 'relatives' and 'the tied-up.'

Chapter 3

Nature and Nostalgia

The second chapter ended with a sense of gloom over political issues. Over the last two decades of Naderpour's life spent in self-imposed exile he wrote some of his best poetry. Sufficient time to reflect on his childhood and youth offered a clearer picture of his life in old age. Equipped with a keener worldview, what he found proved especially depressing. Leaving his homeland surely aggravated such nostalgic feeling. More and more patriotic poems that appear during this reveal that he also pondered the glory of his home country. Multifaceted layers of nostalgia in his later poems at times surface in a single poem. What connects all the poems in this chapter is a sense of pessimism and loss: of childhood, of youth, and of homeland. However, the only safe haven to him was poetry. In the introduction to *Time and Earth* (1996), published four years before his death, he maintained:

> Although man out of necessity gets used to his exile and gradually finds familiarity around him, poetry remains perpetually "heavenly" and will not be polluted with the dust. This heavenly feature of poetry unites contraries, and makes impossible the impossible. The most sinful poem is the purest and the most hopeless one is the herald of hope. Poetry like a breeze passes through everything

> but will not be polluted by anything. It is like the flower that manifests beauty and innocence, in that, in its heavenly texture, it turns the maculate and incompatible particles of soil into a set of beauty and cleanliness. Thus the solid nature of poetry, like that of the flower and the breeze, is a stranger to the contradictory quintessence of the earth and remains an alien in this *dustbin* for ever. (Eidgah 287)

The poem that opens this chapter is "Unstrung." Naderpour divides the ups and downs of life into two halves, the happy days are already gone but the sad parts remain now:

Unstrung

God, happy with His creation,
blessed me with a sitar.

In my lap I pressed its head, like an infant's, on my shoulder,
the two strings fixed on its chest:
two vessels running from the brain to the heart.
I tried both with my fingers,
two melodies were the reply:
one, sad; the other, joyous.
One more pleasant than a drunken sleep in the morning,
the other bitter as the kiss of the lash.
Yet, I set my heart on the lute.
I composed a love song,
pitched high and low out of tune,
neither sad nor happy, but both.
My merry song of old days!
Happy youth, joyous spring!
One night the sky lit up with lightning
like a river consuming its bed.
A great fire rushed into my home,
its ashes blown away with the annihilating wind.
I hung the sitar on a tree
to save it from the fire,
looking at it through the flames
the way a lover looks at his beloved.

At dawn I beheld
its capsized body hanging on a distant branch.
I rushed to it fearful and weeping,
caressing its head in my chest,
clinging so tightly to its sorrowful tune
that I broke the other string.
If there were any joyous melody in the first string
nobody could hear it now.
Now my sitar, a featherless bird, has no cheerful call.

I tell myself, "You delirious man,
from now on just pluck the last string.[1] (*Blood and Ashes*, May, 1987)

LOST CHILDHOOD

Unlike many Western Romantic poets, Naderpour typically avoids writing upon the nuances of childhood experiences. Whereas Wordsworth or Keats might at times seem like innocent children in their poems, Naderpour is primarily interested in the description of adult life. The first poem of his describing an infant, most probably an occasional poem, dates back to early 1965 at the age of thirty-four.[2] Nine years later he composed a poem in a childish atmosphere:

The Flood

I threw a handful of blossoms on water.
A starry sky appeared.

I made a boat out of paper
(as thin as a leaf, as small as a hand)
and a little wax captain
who, like God, sailed the boat away
as far as the blossoms and stars
to undiscovered islands
that he knew by name.

Then a great western storm

capsized the boat;
the captain surrendered his steering
to the waves.

Now there is no God
in my little world.³ (*The Last Supper*, Tehran, June 21, 1974)

However, one has to wait until 1976, when the poet is forty-seven, for him to write in the voice of a child again. In a flashback-like memoir, the speaker in "The Diary" summarizes his life span on a day trip where he lands upon the sun's plane. Meticulously chosen images represent different stages of life from childhood to old age. A pun employed consciously by Naderpour is the word *shahr*, 'city' in Persian but 'month' in Arabic. Thus, the dominant time imagery of a day acquires new bearing. Another example of this word play is in another poem that comes before "The Diary" in *The Last Supper*. It is titled, "The Month of Ramadan" and opens thus: "The city is visible from the rooftop."

The Diary

The sun's golden aircraft
turned full circle
and came in for a landing.
At the airport, I walked off with Dusk.
Young trees on each side of the runway
stood at attention,
welcoming us to the city with cheers.

In the far distance, the guesthouse awaited us;
we walked along the high terrace
that faced the city.
At nightfall, Dusk said goodbye.

Then the spirit of the night
(that drunk walking specter)
awoke within me.
I stepped, with his legs, into the street.

Nature and Nostalgia

"What time is it, sir?" I asked a hurried passer-by.
"A minute past noon," he replied.
(it was the start of the evening).
"Which noon, the one dividing life?" I asked.

I stared at the faces of strangers,
ancient associates, neighbors
in the distant city of my youth,
a city as you already know.[4]

But I saw with my own eyes
under all the skin,
Time, the portraitist,
sketching their old countenances.

In the book-seller's alley,
a drunk man with glasses
scanned titles, his spectacles
lifting lines to his mind.

I saw a worn out calendar
engraved on his head,
the end of days, catastrophic nights,
and thoughts of destiny.

Under a streetlight, an old prostitute,
broken like her wineglass
stared at me. Behind her eyes
a young virgin stood watching.

A man approached, pressing a child
to his chest, his plump body tucked
into his paltry shadow
and within that shadow
the child awoke from sleep.

I passed through the distant city of youth
with a suitcase of memories;
after midnight, I came home with my specter.

On the threshold, he said goodnight.

The next morning the sun's golden aircraft
prepared for takeoff.
I went to the airport
but the young trees
no longer stood at attention,
nor did they chant an anthem
because this time a stranger named Dawn
walked beside me,
and they knew me only
as a friend of Dusk. (The Last Supper, Paris, October 11, 1976)

A similar poem, "Perspective," follows this one five years later. It is another one of his childhood poems that combine remorse on the passage of life and nostalgic feelings for the lost treasure of childhood, youth and homeland. The poet skillfully sets in order a microcosmic journey of the sun—morning, noon, and evening—and connects it to a macrocosmic one of childhood, youth, and old age. This is not, of course, a new technique, since Keats follows a similar pattern in "To Autumn." In the first stanza images of morning as birth, in the second noontime as maturity, and in the third evening as death thread through much of the poem.

Perspective

1

I can still remember the mountain at whose foot
the god of evening was scattering a handful of stars in his grass

to reap bounteous light in the morning.

I stand at an open window facing the sky,
the horizon a mirror

broader than the sea.

In this endless lucid night

Nature and Nostalgia

I repeat lost years of childhood
in my old age.

2

In the mirror a child appears
who from his small bedroom in twilight
sees the red paw of the sun on the mane of the mountain
combing his black hair with a golden brush.

The child who, in the fever of the sun,
considers the tulip more scorching than an oven;
He longs to throw the dough of his imagination into its mouth
and feed butterflies with bread.

In his eyes green honey bees
are the world's winged flowers;
he wants to animate all the flowers in the garden
with fluttering wings.

He forces the noonday sun to gaze at the grasshopper
with a magnifying glass,
to give away spots onto this earth-bird
to match the butterfly.

On the farm
he makes a small aqueduct

through the slippery anthills
to quench thirst of the ants.[5]

In his eyes
blossoms on trees are spring snow
to shake it off completely
before the rain.

Always a mutual understanding between him and the willows,
he firmly presses their delicate hands
to show the heat of his affection.
But always thirstier than the sun

he presses his teeth to freshly washed leaves,
chewing off their bright green enamel
—like the whites and yolks of daffodils
or the redness of raspberries—
and from the bitterness of truth
and sweetness of imagination
he gives his tongue and mind
innumerable tastes and colors.

3

In the mirror a child appears
dragging his blind shadow after himself
to the village spring
to immerse, before sunset, that perplexed barefooted boy
in running water.

He then greets the twilight
and on the roof of the house finds the night
in the mosquito net of the galaxy,
stars—the earth's baby teeth—reflected in the garden pond.
He imagines the call of frogs and crickets
as the conversation of evil spirits and fairies.
He deemed far trees
unknown ghosts.

4

The mountain at whose foot
the god of evening was scattering a handful of stars in his grass
to reap bounteous light in the morning
remains far from the land of my loneliness.

Tonight, under the lamp memories,
stars pour from heaven on my face,
my eyes blinded with tears. (*False Dawn*, August 19, 1981)

"A Future in the Past," "Time and Earth," "A Voyage from the End to the Beginning," "Birth of a Star," and "Blood and Nail"—all listed below chronologically—remain in the same mood with a bleaker tonal difference in later poems. In "Birth of a Star," white hair takes the speaker back to his infancy, so he calls himself a "milk-and-sugar-haired old child" and ironically congratulates the union of the old baby to both cradle and grave. In "A Future in the Past," there is microcosmic and macrocosmic journey similar to the one in "Perspective." However, instead of focusing on the span of a single day, the voyage microcosmically covers a year, starting from spring through winter to represent a human journey.

> A Future in the Past
>
> That village at the edge of the Alborz Mountains—
> extending to the sun from the east
> and to the moon from the west—
> became my childhood geography,
> teaching me the approach of morning and evening
> with the luster of the dawn on its walls
> and the dance of white poplar leaves and branches
> in the fiery twilight.
> When the new spring showed the rise of blossoms
> in the Nowruz sky,[6]
> when the Christ-like sun
> blew a young soul into the mass of old trees and rejuvenated them
> I dashed out of the cottage.
> In the yawning wind of village alleyways,
> I lived on the smell of dust.
> The hive of the city, on the back of distant hills
> became my imaginative playground:
> sometimes, golden pigeons,
> like a small train of bees
> pleased with their soaring;
> sometimes, parallel minarets,
> like twin bright antennas
> on the back of a snail-like dome
> at a far-reaching vista.
> When moon arrows set on fire
> dawn's furnace in the feverish night,
> I yearned for aromatic spearmint

in the folds of oat bread.
I spat out the sweat plum stones
stuck in my teeth
at thirsty noon.
With passionate kisses,
I warmed the soft and lustful cheeks of apple
in red twilight.

When dispersed flocks
returned home from ranches,
when dusty cattle
hung steaming dung buckets
on the ground
with the rope of their tails
from upside down wells,[7]
I competed with the frogs'
nighttime songs,
beating the rhythm
on the bowl of the horizon.

When the troops of autumn approached
from memory's rooftops,
I saw red and yellow sycamore leaves,
like colorful panes of the public bath.[8]

When the cold winter wind
at dawn
hennaed the fingertips of the shepherd girl,
when the milk of light from the sun's breast
flowed into the copper sky,
The Alborz[9] mountains neighed before me.
I became an adventurous knight
facing the light of future.

Now I am sitting on the western strand,
no future light in front,
no sun to guide me within.
I escaped home but Time's wrath
punished me at the night of my exile.

I look at my soil from a distance
with no trace of my footprints
in its gloomy sky. The day is dead.
What use are my prayers after this?
Where is the green land of my childhood?
There remains no flowering home[10] to put on its soil
for my laughs to bloom again.
My village, once alive, is in ruins.
Where is the Alborz,
neighing in the snow,
to bring me the news of kings?
The sound of his sad moaning
seems lost in my soundless crying.
Alas, the morning rider will step down from his high stirrup
not in my house.
The evening sun has pushed my great future
like a shadow
behind me .... (Blood and Ashes, August, 1984)
Time and Earth

In my home village a big stream
flowed through dusty and silent alleyways:
the water was as clear as raindrops,
and through dense heaps of thorny bushes and stones
carolling happily
passed with the spring breeze
in a sunny depth. The color of pebbles
(with rays of azure, orange, and aquamarine)
had woven a tapestry.

The big stream in my home village
Under the silver light in dawn:
animating the images of migratory pigeons
–through poplar branches–
on its wavy surface
like a cloth pattern.
On gloomy rainless days:
the image of the dishevelled hair of clouds
in henna coloured claws of sycamore

or the image of vitreous spider trap
(with bright morning dewdrops
on shiny and coarse wings of flies)
among the dense green branches
showed on its clean tablet
and that clear current
tight in its bosom
on both ends
in constant and gentle intercourse
with wild spearmint and old roots:
soaked into earth's cavities
and hid behind stones.
And then, set off again for distant lands
quiet and unhurried.
The big stream in my home village
looked like the stream of "Time"
that through life's clear memories
(with azure, orange, and aquamarine colors)
heavier and thicker than honey
–in Paradise–
opened a way to future lands.

Now, the same clear current
in hard cement ditches,
flows fast as wind and lightning
away from the our lonely land: the aged
flows not through plants and stones
and on the way refuses to slant toward memory,
no longer stopping behind roots
or before Spearmint
and no longer fearing any Dead Leaf.
Here, Time and Memory
flee from each other,
as day from night.

In this land
(in loneliness as vast as waiting and sorrow)
we migrate to Time's destruction
with no relish,

with no relic. (Time and Earth, September 1993)

A Voyage from the End to the Beginning

Those burning bitter coffees
and those dispersed circles of smoke
on the counters of the rendezvous
in the distant city of youth.

That childlike heart of the clock
on the naked chest of the wall
and that beating clock
behind my shirt
both enthusiastic about the moment of meeting
at the height of concealed anxiety.

That first big kiss
on thirsty crimson lips
with laughter as far reaching as the waves
on a face as fair as water
at the moment as you already know it.[11]

That sound of footsteps walking together
in calm and dusty alleyways,
and that tête-à-tête of the cricket with the moon
from among tree leaves
in a long and breathtaking sentence
with a dreadful stammer.

Those distant old memories,
those old torn out photos
set out among the whirlwind of events
for the lost land
for shores
no one will ever know.

Now I am in this wonderful fancy
upon the annihilation of the quicksilver of existence,
the clear mirror of my mind

exhausting memory's pictures
like the blue western sky
of autumn's yellow sun.

Then on that night of oblivion
I am the century's old infant
who out of bad luck remembers nothing
but the poignant memory of birth
with a loud cry
in the bed of universal silence.... *(Earth and Time,* August, 1995)

Birth of a Star

Strange gaze in the mirror,
behind my dark hair of puberty
thoughts of the morning sun,
arose within me.

Today in my old age
the sun still shines on my head,
but true thoughts rising within me
shadow this false dawn.

Night flows into consciousness,
a long dangerous way
to the indifferent mirror:
from bright adolescent dawn
to the evening of senility.

Strange gaze in the mirror,
tomorrow my image becomes
a baby reborn
into a foreboding dawn.
This milk-and-sugar-haired old child
emerges from a mother as bitter as the night,
preparing for a more unpleasant life to come
of a night of dark solitude.

Congratulations on the unexpected meeting

of this baby
with both cradle and grave.
Wonderful night,
congratulations
on the birth of this star! (*False Dawn*, March 1981)

"Blood and Nail" is the antepenultimate poem in Naderpour's last book, *Time and Earth*. In a nutshell it recaps the story of life and death. It is based on a word play on *khun* 'blood' and *nâkhun* 'nail.' However, the negative prefix *nâ* creates a word in the mind of native speakers of Persian similar to 'unblood,' so the title can be reworded or retranslated as "Blood and Unblood" to perhaps make better sense. This image is further reinforced when at the beginning of the poem, at first blood, then wine, and afterwards a baby nurtured with mother's milk is introduced. However, the speaker sees blood and milk oozing out of the nails on fingers and toes as if life is flowing out of the body. The image of scissors at the end of the poem is apt since the speaker, while cutting the nails, is pondering on how blood and milk have produced life as he now cuts life away in a suicidal frenzy.

Blood and Nail

From the crystal bowl on the horizon

I drink the living blood from my dead past
more readily than old home-made wine.
And from its black intoxication
I suddenly forget myself and sleep
in the privacy of night;
but if the thick milk in the baby's body,
thanks to the nurturing of his mother,
turns into blood,
then the blood in my old body
turns back into milk,
turns my thoughts whiter than baby hair
peeping from my finger tips or toes.
The blood and milk

have mixed nails and daylight
into the darkness of my being;
The blood of twilight,
as white as milk, drops on my fingers
and leaves a stain.
Afraid of falling onto the ground,
it congeals in the winter
that I've come to embody.

When the night begins to darken the sky,
I recall the living blood of my youth
and the fiery scissors
cutting me from the world
to which I once belonged. (*Time and Earth*, October, 1995)

Lost Youth

Naderpour's obsession with the passage of time in many of his poems is common in many middle-aged people. "The Red Lamp of Anemone" is an early poem recounting the anxiety of a middle-aged man confronting the passage of time. As early as 1970 when he was forty-one, he was preoccupied with the question of aging, so he went to his favorite trope of the personification of nature and flowers to count the ticks of the clock:

The Red Lamp of Anemone

Copper-colored like twilight,
time taught me to tarnish.

I spent my life knocking on the door of hope
without an answer.
He taught me to knock on another door.

I took the red lamp of anemone
as companion on my voyage
and went to welcome Dawn
who taught me to stay still.
Now, dreaming of a voyage,

sitting, like a knocker on the door,
I am going nowhere,
unsure.

I am happy with the clock's hands
triumphantly slipping by.
In mirrors there is an old man
staring into me,
staring

Into me.... (*From the Sublime*, Tehran, June 16, 1970)

The Last Supper (1978) contains poems concerned with loss and infidelity. The poet borrows the title from religion in order to convey not only a sense of betrayal but also the termination of something finite. He finds both these issues in the passage of life. Like "The Flood" and "The Diary," the following poems from this book are most representative of the whole collection:

The Last Supper

From the beaches of an unknown night
the wind spread the odor
of men's roasted bodies
on our tablecloth.
We toasted our glasses, but within us
the bottle of faith had shattered.

None of us looked the other in the eye.
Our mouthfuls of blood
were gulping back tears
as we sobbed to ill-timed
spasms of laughter.

In a night when the kiss smacked of betrayal,
we burnt the kind and vigorous face of the friend
encircled by a divine halo
with a tongue redder than flames;

we sold our love for the kiss of hatred.

With the rough immoral stone
at the enemy's infernal gallows,
we injured Hallaj who shouted the truth,[12]
we transferred power from our saints to Yazid;[13]
more pious than all the impure, we
dipped our fingernails into our friend's blood.

We put the high stool of thought
like Aristotle's nine suspending spheres
under the lame feet of flattery.
We built towers out of skulls.
We wrote of our conquests on shrouds.

We, the blind-eyed, bruise
looking for essential wisdom,
rubbed fingers blinder than hearts
on embossed words and lines
to read the names of the most crooked[14]
raised higher than moles upon idolized beloveds.

We built adobe houses on water.[15]
We threw stones at mirrors;
Like Arabs of old, wandering in the wilderness,
we dug graves for honorable girls
in the salty waste land of ignorance.

We carried our dead on our shoulders;
we sowed and reaped
grains of tears and sweat
in farms of fear and shame;
we forced the spirit to serve the body.[16]

In the casino of history
we lost our legacy of ancient generations,
the same way we had already lost our fame.
We tasted our captivity in time

as if from a bottle.

No sign of dawn in the sky.
The deep wound of the sun's dagger,
like an old keepsake from the distant past,
burnt our cold hearts.
The plant of our salvation
decayed with incessant rain.

We picked up crumbs from the earth's table.
We dipped pieces of our friend's body
in bowls of blood;
In the black Iscariotic night
we were guests at the Last Supper. (*The Last Supper*, August 15, 1974)

In "Picture Pause" the speaker is frightened to find his picture in a mirror that is mocking his clock. In Persian there is meaningful harmony in the title *maks-e-aks* since a picture is immobile as if life has stopped. The speaker is petrified to imagine his picture turned into a fossil.

Picture Pause

No doubt the mirror watchfully
scorns my clock's circling.

With every motion of the hand,
a line in the mirror depicts the minutes' dance.

A spectrum of repeated images
stretches between two poles of profile and face,
multiplying my picture.

In the mirror's vivid stare, I find myself as I am:
clothed like dawn's hope in the universal night,
more naked than the birth of a sun,
raw as whatever the creator has made in the tree,
perfect as his craftsmanship.

> The mirror's gaze interprets such fated dualism.
>
> I reflect what will happen
> if this picture in the mirror
> suddenly gets harder than a fossil
> in the heart of the earth.
> This evil vision ages me. (*The Last Supper*, Tehran, August 17, 1974)

In "Punishment," Naderpour goes back to his favorite images borrowed from nature to denote death and annihilation. The speaker finds himself in the grip of fate. The perpetual fighting of day and the counting of numbers have a striking resemblance to Edgar Allan Poe's short story "The Masque of the Red Death." In Prince Prospero's court the courtiers and the prince himself are doomed to die one by one as the ebony clock ticks on. But the Red Death will be hanged at 'sunrise." Here the speaker aligns himself with the day in a duel whose two main players, night and day, are in a perpetual fight.

> Punishment
>
> The judge of the heavens,
> to eradicate enemies of the night
> in his court of Balkh,[17]
> sentences me and the day to death
> for living boldly.
> In the twilight we're moved to the firing squad
> at the rifle range called Dusk
> where the angels of justice
> ceremonially blindfold us with the handkerchief of memory[18]
> despite our insistence on leaving our eyes open.
> The sun with his red pistol
> counts one, two, three, four, five....
> We lean against the courage of the wall.
> The gun fires on seven.
> As the pale day falls down,
> I ran away through fire and blood.
> The sun, who missed the mark,
> remains as perplexed as me.

After this, we both wait for our punishment
like two mirrors standing before each other.
Tomorrow night the sun is taken
from the heavenly court of Balkh
straight to the firing squad:
He leans against the ruthlessness of the wall.
Night, with his pistol
repeats the counting of one, two three, four, five.... (*False Dawn*,
September, 1981)

Old age has been commonly associated with winter and Naderpour is no exception. In "To the Mirror" the speaker finds himself bent double under the load of days, eyes filled with darkness and hair whitened by snow. The word whisper is aptly used to perpetually remind the speaker of the sad fact of life.

To the Mirror

The snowy days fell so heavily
my hair turned to winter.
What day's rain might wash away
all this white?

Night filled my eyes with such darkness
that these bright springs went dry.
What water now reflects
the rising sun?

The days lean on my shoulders so heavily
that I double over.
Someone now whispers:
"The weight of your sins hunches your back."

At the end of my life I know
that morning's mirror sees my dark eyes.
Can it grant me one last strand of black
in the mass of white hair? (*Time and Earth*, December, 1989)

The thought of death is so frightening that it turns the aging speaker into a maniac in "Footstep." All the images employed in the poem are negative: desert, drunk, unaware, devil, out of sight, masked sun, highwayman, and death. The double motif haunts Naderpour with trauma in some other poems like "There is Someone in Me," "A Man with Two Shadows," "The Invisible Twin," "The Naked Masked Figure," and "Panic," all of which appear in *Time and Earth*.

Footstep

In a wide desert
through the dead of night
a heavy footstep
follows my shadow.

Frightened, I turn around
to find the wind and a tree:
one drunk, the other unaware.

Who in the devil is it? I ask.
Who is out of sight?

No reply from the vacant desert.
The mountain hides behind the trees.
I only hear
heavy footsteps of someone nearby.

As I keep searching in vain,
the moon on the horizon
looks like a masked sun
wandering in the heart of night
like a highwayman
(my evening traveling companion
toward eternity).

Fallen shadow,
if you stick by me until sunrise
you will find, on the ground,

thousands of night footsteps
outnumbering my first footprints
made in the morning.
These hints will tell you
this being whose footsteps you fear
is death in the form of another day. (*Time and Earth*, November, 1991)

In the poem, "Point and Line," the speaker defies his old knowledge of geometry by giving a new definition of a straight line. Here there is a challenge of theory and experience in which the speaker goes for the latter. The poem is reminiscent of Walt Whitman's "When I heard the Learn'd Astronomer" in which the speaker goes for experiencing nature directly rather than understanding it through figures and numbers.

Point and Line

Under the high blue ceiling of a distant sky,
in the city of scattered memories,
on the day when a breeze blew
from one classroom window
through another,
the old geometry teacher drew a white line
from two points on the black board,
saying, "The shortest distance between two points
—like the breeze between these two windows—
is a straight line."[19]

Today my experience disproves that theory.
The long journey of my unfinished life
strays far from a straight line between two points;
This terrifying path
from birth to death
—lightning in a dark night—
looks more like a scattered line
drawn on the ground
with the finger

from a stranger's hand. (*Time and Earth*, October, 1993)

"Snapshot" is a quick image of probably a real experience of the poet at the seaside in a small bar. The poet, attracted by the beauty of a young dancing girl who very soon disappears from the speaker's sight, is left alone in disappointment. The speaker finds a similarity between the incident and the way in a blink of an eye youth left him while he was not sober. The title and the incident emphasize the suddenness of the events.

Snapshot

A dark winter night in a little bar
on the coast of a western land;
rain crying in the distance,
and inside, the guitar's laughter amidst so much commotion,
and aromatic smoke through the brain of the meningitic chandelier,
and the cold metal counter in the hands of the drunk,
and the sleepy dance of the curtain before those still awake,
and the magical presence of a lonely girl before those drifting into dreams,
and her wet lips in the ecstasy of fire
and I, dying to talk to her
and she, close to the mob of strangers, far from my kind glances,
and her sudden escape from this place
and her dear name, "Youth," still on my tongue. (*Time and Earth*, February, 1994)

The motif of alter ego appears in "American Night," but this time the speaker notices that his company is someone else, even though they pace together. He comes to a conclusion that in the city of angels gods of light and darkness are paradoxically the same.

American Night

The place of my exile:
a city on the western coast
with old pines and new palaces[20]

Nature and Nostalgia

taller than giants.

Though in the greedy eyes of residents of the earth
this city looks like the home of angels,
it remains a beautiful hell,
having admitted the devil
at the origin of the world.
Those living here forget the fate
of their ancestors and long
for forbidden fruit.

This evening,
the old sun in his delirious fever
jumped from the highest skyscraper
onto the sea rocks
but the tall windows of the city
refused to see his black death,
waiting, as if for a miracle,
from the east.

After his death,
the stars in the lonely night
hid their delicate sparkling
within the warm clouds of smoke
and small raindrops as clean
as pigeons' eyes.

In a night blacker than marble,
I walk on a carpet of autumn leaves,
staring at passing birds
as tears drip from heaven
into my eyes
until everything—stones, animals, and humans—
begins to drown.

From the autumn wind
I drink the smell of dust
like bitter wine
in memory of my motherland

and start crying.
This time my eyes
see clearly through tears
pictures of numerous city lights
floating on stagnant rain water.

Among the hum of wet branches
through empty alleyways
I find my path home,
upset by a passing stranger's footstep
following me through
the heart of the night;
my company
is not one and the same as me
though we pace together.

Suddenly,
above distant trees
the wind disperses the black clouds,
and the night maliciously unveils
the face of the moon
to reveal a masked bandit;
I stare at his pistol
and find that in the city of angels
Ahriman and Ahura are the same.[21] (*Time and Earth*, December, 1994)

The last poem in Naderpour's last book in Persian, *Time and Earth*, is "Clock Hand and Scorpion." As expected it concerns death and fatalism. The speaker starts a conceit by playing on the Persian and Arabic words *aqrab,* 'scorpion' and *aqrabak,* 'clock hand.' He recalls childhood amusement of placing a scorpion in a circle of fire and the speckle of its suicide. He finds a clock's hand in a similar inescapable 'vicious circle' and suggests that it's suicide. There is an indirect sense of fatalism in the simile, since one recalls Shakespeare's *King Lear* in which one reads, "As flies to wanton boys, are we to the gods./ They kill us for their sport."

Nature and Nostalgia

Clock Hand and Scorpion

Behind the window of memories wet with rain
a circle of fire started by a neighbor child
under an old sycamore in my front yard
still burns.

Returning from the desert day
to the village night,
he taught the scorpion
that looked like a toy
to dance with death
in this bright circle.

The scorpion, fearing an untimely death,
walked back and forth, between thirst and fire,
slipping so many times
that it lost all its energy,
casting its own venomous tail
out of desperate rage
on its own useless being,
closing its greedy eyes
to the world
as it burned
in this bright circle.

Clock hand, every day I see you
indifferent to life
within the transparent glass case
and the heart's ring of numbers;
no matter how hard you beat
on time's door
there's no escaping this tiny circle;
fearing consciousness, you're better off casting your tail—
full of venomous boredom—
onto yourself,
falling into an intoxicating sleep
where noon feels like midnight
as you stop counting "moments."

> Killed in the fiery circle like the scorpion,
> you'd finally stop trying to measure
> the infinite mystery. (*Time and Earth*, January 15, 1996)

Lost Land

Naderpour was not a patriotic poet. Especially in his youth, he did not celebrate his native country in his verse. However, there are a few fine poems that do address his home country, especially the Old Persian Empire, with requisite rhetorical gusto. However, there is a change in his choice of subjects when he living abroad and feels homesick. There are two poems written when he was still in his country and the rest take place when he was abroad. "Petition," addressed to the Caspian Sea, is full of literary tropes and polysemy in Persian like a play on the Arabic word *bahr* meaning 'sea' and 'poetical scale' since they were as extensive as the sea. The Persian title *Arizeh* used to be a petition to an authority usually a ruler. At the beginning there were usually a number of flattering apostrophes to ensure that the intended request would be met. Similarly, the poet finds the sea a source of power and authority making pledges to it.

> Petition
>
> You fluent green!
> You impossible simplicity!
> You sacred script written on the silk night!
> You Holy Verse inscribed on the dawn.
> You hymn acclaiming the four seasons!
> You open book of heaven's epithets!
>
> You on whose wave of Persian letters, every bird becomes a dot!
> You whose every drop becomes a sign in the message from a cloud.
> You whose sorrowful absence and eventful presence
> becomes a momentary story on the shore.
>
> You eloquent green!

You extended opening of a lyric!
You profound meaning of an epic!
You birthplace of the word "sun"!
You rising meter of the moon's rhyme![22]
You sign of smooth and easeful expression!

You body of metrical waters!
You spot for words' collusion!
You dervishes' dance![23]
You knotting and unknotting of speech!
You meaning of breaking meters!
You periodic brilliant sentence (between western and eastern crescents)![24]
You union of jungle with mountain and galaxy!

You capsized city with inverted inscriptions
full of ups and downs,
covered with outlines and sketches of stars!
You green suspended heavens!
You Sassanid monument in Kermanshah![25]

You, verse! You boiling essence with more fluid than the magic sap of life in a tree's root!
Saturate me with the echo of your call!
You lion, roaring with your mane blowing in a wind-storm,
pull down my body, quench my soul!
Rip and tear my trachea!

Pull off my subjugating shackles!
And smash this agitated rowboat of my being
on the sun's golden rock!
You deep, you high, you dread, you threat,
you green, you Caspian Sea! (*The Last Supper*, Tehran, April 21, 1974)

Three months before the victory of the revolution he composed another poem "Lyric 2" for his country. However, there is a marked difference between the two in that in the latter he felt prematurely nostalgic for a country which he was going to leave forever. He prophetically foresaw that he would not be able to live happily anywhere else.

Lyric 2

Ancient land, beloved land!
I separated my heart from you,
but where should I stay?

No energy to go, no patience to remain;
how should I put it? I am a dry tree.
No wonder if the woodcutter covets my bones.

In this hell, how can a heavenly flower
blossom or smell?
Spring! How can I benefit from April's clouds
when I myself am the fall?

The grandeur of old age, decreed by God, would not suit me.
I secretly listened to the devil whispering that I am young.

The silence of falsehood killed
the voice of truth in the dead of the night.
Now a secret sorrow will torment me
until the Day of Resurrection.

Departing pigeons will not call at my roof
to bring the message
in a friend's handwriting.
The ship of the heart is drifting with no coast light visible;
In this dark no dawn appears.

Do help me, O God;
is it possible to open a door and let out the sorrow?

I will skin the black night with nails and teeth
to get the bloodstained naked morning
across the threshold of my sky.

Ancient land, beloved land!

Intending to go, I separated my heart from you yet
I cannot live anywhere but here. (*False Dawn*, Tehran, November 10, 1978)

The two poems cited above were simply about the poet's home country, but after he left the country he added a new facet to his patriotic poems by making constant comparisons between the west and the east. In "Under a Western Sky," he points out that in the West "time is gold" and things are based on a "profit-and-loss" basis. As for nature, "Sunset has the color of lunacy/ Rain sounds like crying in solitude/ Stars have all gone blind." Atypical for Naderpour, he does not mention where he composed the poem; perhaps in a city of exile it did not matter where he was. What mattered to him was that he was not at home and that he was "under a Western sky."

Under a Western Sky

Tonight I hear your footsteps
from the alleys of memory.
Have you, dear distant one,
come to this city of loneliness?

Here the birds of dawn
flying overhead
leave me yearning for heaven.
But at night
walls remind me of a secret captivity.
How would you find me here?
I know no one among these strangers
except myself;
my picture is imprisoned in a mirror.
I stand gazing before this image,
preferring not to sit next to others.

Here you will find me in a mirror
which is like a clock
whose hidden hands
circle profit-and-loss,

a cruel business mind
dimming my appearance
with minutes and seconds.
Here time is gold:
every moment a priceless elixir.
But I am the indifferent calendar of days and nights.
Sunset has the color of lunacy.
Rain sounds like crying in solitude.
Stars have all gone blind.

Here I will not go beyond the window;
the opposite wall is a border closed to visitors.
Here a neighbor's lamp will not attract my eyes.
Alienation has become my best friend.

In this country doors always open inwards.
In the sad land of my solitude,
under the foggy western sky,
night lives in my heart,
and day breaks from my gray temples.

Here there is no sad stranger like me,
and no light of certitude in the delusions of night,
only the sound of a wandering heart,
the call of a perplexed passerby's footstep
ringing in the alleys of memory.
Dear distant one,
behind what door or tree are you standing?
Have you come to the city of my loneliness? (*False Dawn*, May 1981)

In "Sunrise in the West," Naderpour returns to his favorite imagery of nature. The poem is included in the *False Dawn*, which is based on light and darkness imagery. Images of fire, the sun, and Zoroastrianism are juxtaposed with those of darkness and evening in the West. The poet constantly remembers the old light and doubted if he would see his country once again. The same images appear in another poem addressed

Nature and Nostalgia

to Damavand, the highest mount in Iran in "A Winter Oration." The poet nostalgically wishes for another visit to the mount.

    Sunrise in the West

    In my homeland
    the sun fails to appear
    after the rising blood.
    A red moonlight from the eastern horizon
    shines on burnt faces
    and imitates the lost sun,
    but still behind that white peak[26]
    the Sun lives in the form of a Simorgh.[27]
    One day, unexpectedly, I find
    its shadow above me.
    Now in this Christian land
    I stand on the threshold of my exile:
    the Night, above church spires
    crucifies every single star,
    but some light from the western horizon
    spurs on the icy sky
    threatening the east from a distance.
    I know my lost sun does not bring this dusk-like rise.
    I witness the sunrise through the night
    in other lands and horizons.[28]

    It seems I am returning to the beginning of the world
    and out of the two fires at the beginning of the cosmos
    one shines in this new rising,
    but how to tell which one?
    That flame still punishing
    vultures' beaks and the thief's liver?
    That beautiful burning
    as a miraculous lamp in that black night
    stolen from the high mount of gods
    to guide the earthly man to sparkling morn?
    Or a fire that was the pride of the angel
    but turned into the proof of human misery?
    That fire of arrogance that made Satan

an enemy of mankind[29]
to expel him from Paradise to the Earth?
Which one shall I see in the evening of life:
that blessed light that shone on the earth
to help us rise to heaven
or the sparkle of that spite that made us fall
from the expanse of heaven to the constraints of earth,
growing roots in the dustbin like trees?
No answer to my question.
This new sun in western horizons
is nothing more than an impression of my eastern sun.
O, you distant land!
You land of my childhood!
May the cold western sun be forbidden to me
as long as your sun exists in the horizons of my mind!
You remembered soil!
You immortal relief of days!
You who are cleaner, more lucid than water and mirror!
Everywhere, I behold my own image in you.
As long as I have eyes on you, I fail to see inside myself.
You gilded palace!
You cerulean rooftop of history!
The lantern of your memory
remains eternally burning in my dreams
under the roof of exile,
the sparkle of your dream
that, at the time my weeping,
beams through my cloudy morning.
Here your brightness is my everlasting guide.
You birthplace of Mithras and of love[30]
You manifestation of Zoroaster's fire!
Though the night stands before me
I am fortunate[31] that my eyes turn toward you
and from behind the earth's foggy mountains
my star becomes visible in your morning sky.
You kingdom of never-ending days!
You ancient land of youth,
You ancient nest to Simorgh!
One day, unannounced,

when I look out of the window at the sky
I will see your sun before me.... (*False Dawn*, July, 1981)

The last poem chosen in this chapter comes from *Blood and Ashes*. It is the story of the homeless, one literary, and the other figuratively. The speaker meets a native drunkard who begs a penny from him but in his eyes finds his own image whose state looks no better than the drunkard's.

A Spring Tale

I told myself, "You who have lost your land!
Why do you recoil from the world?
What did you get from your country out of so much eternal longing?

"This city of loneliness is your home.
Live here as you did in your own land;
if you shed blood tears
don't look on the bloody soil!

"If the wheel turns against your will
take revenge on it![32]
If it did not make you happy in your own country
enjoy life in a foreign land!

"Stroll out at night,
drink a cup of twilight-colored wine,
leave the bridle of reason with inebriation
and forget about life's sorrows!

"Out of so many beautiful ones around you
take one as your beloved
and as the ancients advised
get caught in the chain of her hair!

"Imagine no one under the blue
but you and her
and that you own the night.

Just drink and indulge your pleasures!"

Having heard all this,
the heart breaks open,
the world turns beautiful
as time passes peacefully.

It was still daylight
when I, clean shaven,
taught my lips to smile
as I dressed in fine clothes.

I left so content
that sorrow felt ashamed.
The breeze blew so violently
it disheveled my hair.

No sooner had I taken a few steps among the crowd
when a ragged old beggar stopped me
with an empty bottle in hand,

asking for extra change , which I gave him.
He looked at me thanklessly,
leaving me to reflect
the empty gratitude in his eyes.

Suddenly the spring cloud started crying,
wetting the ground with God's pure tears.
I stared at that filthy beggar
and he grinned.

His mirroring eyes revealed
that I was as ragged as him.
I found no living soul
before or behind him.

He and I, two lost homeless men:
one drunk, the other sober:
the spring night mocked

our weeping clothes.

As dusk emerged from behind the clouds
and the old man left nothing but a vague remembrance
from the clamor of the crowd in that busy alley
nothing was heard but the moan of a storm drain.

I told myself, "You who have lost your land!
even a shadow refuses to follow you.
Do not turn down this eternal loneliness
as your future will be no better than your present.

"How can one who did not benefit from the past,
expect anything better from future?"
The dusk was half-living, the night arriving.
In the laughter of the world flowed a bitter tear. (*Blood and Ashes*, May, 1982)

Notes

1. In modern Persian the idiomatic expression is more in vogue than the literal meaning of 'plucking the last string'; it means 'doing some bold and dangerous action as one's last chance, especially when one is desperate.'
2. "Infant" appears in Chapter 4.
3. A play on *khodâ*, 'god,' and *nâkhodâ*, 'ship captain.'
4. An allusion to an anecdote in a chapter concerning youth and the passage of life by a thirteenth century Persian poet, Saadi.
5. The child is apparently quenching the thirst of the ants while in reality he is drowning them.
6. March 21, the first day on the Persian calendar.
7. A beautiful way of seeing an unpleasant act of defecation.
8. Unlike the poem, "To Autumn," here everything related to nature is beautiful and simple because in the poet's eyes, they are juxtaposed with Western life.
9. Alborz Mount; a masculine name as well.
10. In Persian *gel*, 'mud,' and *gol*, 'flower,' are spelled the same but sound different. Thus, there is an association of 'bloom' with 'adobe.'
11. Here Naderpour in a footnote refers the reader to Saadi who is already alluded to in "The Diary."
12. Hussein bin Mansur, nicknamed Al-Hallaj, a famous Sufi leader in tenth century, was executed for the blasphemy of saying "I am the Truth," i.e. "I am God." That is the final stage of the Sufi journey but it makes no sense to a literalist. In a footnote, Naderpour refers to this story from Attar Neyshabouri's *Biography of God's Friends* (13 century). Throughout the poem themes of godliness and saintliness are juxtaposed with inhumanity and treason of us humans.
13. There are many figures in history that go by the name of Bayazid. Some were rulers and one is a famous Sufi, exemplary for saintliness. Yazid, son of Muawiyah ordered Prophet Mohammad's grandson, Hussein, to be killed. So the adjective Yazidi means 'ruthlessness' in the Shia sect. The poet plays on the names Bayazid and Yazid while they are diametrically different in connotations. Thus there is degeneration from the zenith of divinity to the nadir of meanness and brutality.
14. *Haft khat*, 'seven-lined,' is an idiomatic expression for a charlatan. Now the poet plays on seven lines and connects it to Braille readers (in fact

Nature and Nostalgia 99

we are the blind Braille readers) to whom the names of the crooked look more embossed than what we have to really regard important, i.e. raised: the mole of the idols; in Persian classical poetry the mole of idolized beloved is the ultimate of beauty. In short, we mistook bad things for good ones. I was thinking of a word in English to convey "line" and "charlatan." The word 'crooked' came to my mind as it can be used for dishonest people and 'not straight lines.' If you can think of a closer word, please do so. Anyway, the whole imagery in the stanza is beautiful.

15. The original is: "We laid adobe on water" i.e. never drying, and thus a futile endeavor. In the translation I used adobe for adobe houses, in the Persian it is used in its first sense, i.e. sun-dried bricks.
16. The first line of the stanza has the image of burial as does in the previous stanza too. However, here it is related to the mythological (many myths throughout the world) burial of the dead heralding new births. Now as the grain is tear and sweat (our bodies, in the first line of the stanza, are no different from these) nothing beneficial will emerge. The imagery reminds one of T.S. Eliot's *The Waste Land.*
17. Balkh, a city now in Afghanistan, was notorious for its court of injustice. However, the name is a carefully chosen since Balkh is located East of Iran and the birthplace of the sun.
18. The speaker and day see nothing but their memories at the time of death because they are blindfolded by that special handkerchief.
19. [The poets' note] A reference to this line by a Persian poet Sâ'ib Tabrizi (1601/02-1677): "My extinction relies on the breeze of an excuse/ My name is writ on the ground with a fingertip."
20. There is a wordplay on *kâj* 'pine tree' and *kâkh* 'palace.' Depending on the place of the dot above or within the curve of the letter #, the sound of the letter changes.
21. In Zoroastrianism, Ahura Mazda, the deity of light and goodness, is in perpetual battle with his antagonist Ahriman who represents darkness and evil.
22. *Tekyegâh* means a place to rest or lean against as well as the place of the stress in prosody.
23. *Samâ*, the dervishes' dance, means 'hearing.' The second meaning is intended as well.
24. The poet intentionally puts the sentence in parentheses. Helâlein means 'two crescents' as well as 'two parentheses.'

25. A play on *tâqe bostân* 'the Sassanid monument in Kermanshah' and *bâghe bâstân* 'ancient garden.' The Sassanid dynasty ruled in Persia during A.D. 226–651.
26. Damavand, the highest mountain peak in Iran, overlooks Tehran on the east so the sun rises from behind it.
27. A bird in Persian myths, equivalent to phoenix, living on the fabulous Mount Qâf.
28. [The poets' note] A reading of the reappearance of "the leftists" in France and the victory of Socialists in Parliamentary and Presidential elections in 1981.
29. In Persian, as in Hebrew, Adam means both 'man' and 'Adam.'
30. In Persian, *mehr* means both 'Mithras,' god of light, and 'love.'
31. A wordplay on *tâle* meaning, 'rising' and 'fortune, horoscope, lucky star.'
32. In Hafiz there is a similar image: "I will disturb the Wheel if it turns against my will /I am not to be humiliated by Heaven's Wheel."

CHAPTER 4

POET OF PICTURES

Naderpour's skill in producing novel imagery is unique in modern Persian poetry. The irony of Naderpour's case is that he is a master of employing very simple tropes like personification. The variety and novelty of his images remind the English reader of the seventeenth-century English metaphysical poets with their elaborate use of conceits. Another similarity is the association of sensibility, the marriage of thoughts and feelings in many of Naderpour's poems such as "Autumn" or "Infant." Pictorial description dominates Naderpour's thoughts and feelings and his power lies in pure and lively images that are clear and sharp. Naderpour's poems further revive imagistic tradition in an old movement in Persian poetry known as Khoransani.

Such taking to vivid images had pros and cons. The supporters believe that he kindled alive an almost forgotten trend in poetry in modern times. The opponents, however, argue that an image in itself is insufficient and that Naderpour lived in an ivory tower and forgot other people's distress. Forough Farrokhzad (1935–1967), a famous contemporary of Naderpour, criticized him for overemphasis on images and less attention to meaning: "Naderpour's poems are completely devoid of meaning. He is an expert imagist but what is the use of an image alone? What is he going to express with these images? Nothing.... only his own pains impress him" (Eidgah 145). However, had Forough lived until the publication of *False Dawn* and *Time and Earth*, she would have certainly changed her mind. That is why Simin Behbahani, a contemporary poet, divides Naderpour's imagery into two halves: at home (i.e., in his youth) and abroad (i.e., in his maturity). She concurs with Farrokhzad that his images at home were merely superficial, but Behbahani saw the second period of Naderpour's life, as well. For this reason, she argues that the second period reflects images with which the reader can connect (Behbahani 1999). There are critics such as Leonardo Alishan who argue that even in his youth Naderpour was the spokesman of his age:

> Forough Farrokhzad's charge that Naderpour thinks of his pains and sorrows is not true. When Naderpour sold so well in a few years in those times, it means that his sorrows and pains were and still are those of thousands of Iranian readers. The majority of his readers are from the educated middle class and often middle class and fairly well off who somehow suffer from "defective westernization. (Eidgah 356)

In this chapter the selected poems are presented mainly for the imagistic perspectives they offer. Evaluated based on the poems in this chapter, Farrokhzad's charge may seem somewhat valid, though Naderpour should be seen in his entirety rather than just one aspect. The material for Naderpour's novelty in these poems comes from various sources, mainly from nature. An interesting point about the poems selected is that the majority of them were composed when Naderpour was younger. In the last decades of his life, the number of purely imagistic poems decreased. One can speculate upon the reasons. Nostalgic feelings about lost home, childhood, and youth certainly remain a key factor.

Glance

On the glass, the broken spider
had woven a cobweb.
The diamond of your eyes etched a line.

In the silence of trees, the glass shattered.
Now just the moon and your gaze
stare into my eyes.[1] (*The Sun's Kohl*, Tehran, May 5, 1959)

Incident

An astral bird is still flying in the morning's cage;
the night creeps in its snakeskin
leaving me like a passenger stuck in dust.

The dawn's light in the heaven's emerald cup
is milk full of blood clots;
a bird sticks its head out of my bedroom window;
the black snake has shed its skin;
the white bird flown from its cage.
I am surrounded by an incident:
a bird sitting sad in the waves of this dust,
a snake creeping down the path. (*Not Plant*, Tehran, November 30, 1961)

Rome (A Sketch)

Rome: city of empty days, city of long sleep,
city of trees, of obese women, and heavy showers,
Rome: the newest and oldest capital.

Wire threads
through its blue sky
like a spider web.
In its lit alleys,
around midnight,
silence and solitude.

Sometimes, the sound of a kiss off lips
in yellow leaves.
Sometimes, the light through a half-closed window
above a mansion, in the cold sky.

Rome: city of the sun
city of reliefs, and of buildings, and of bells.

Rome: an unmasked city,
city of ruins, and of lawns and stones. (*Not Plant*, Rome, October 22, 1964)

Vista

The snow came and decorated the feast of the day,
filling the night with milky luster,
but how many unbowed trees
were felled under the weight of their arrogance!
How cruel is the cold beauty! (*Not Plant*, Rome, January 1965)

Infant

Eyes: cat's eyes in morning sunlight.
Clenched fists: small sweet figs.
O, blood vessels: in cutaneous enamel more lucid than light,
an amber spider
in the bubble of a grape. (*Not Plant*, Rome, Winter 1965)

From the Train Window

The train crawled across the ground
like a small silkworm.
The desert, wet and green,
like a mulberry leaf;
in the distance,
like children in a chain
hills ran towards the horizon.
Each had planted a torch of stars
on the sharp sticks of far trees
that cut through the darkness.
The moon's white ball

in the mountain's two hands
seemed confused.
The train, panting and chugging,
gradually reached
the end of the desert. (*Not Plant*, Tehran, August 1957)

Narrative

The black hen brooded the white egg,
telling the embryo beating within,
"Look, you eyeball! My womb of lime
is not a dark cell;
it's full to the brim
with the simplicity of dawn.
The sun sleeps in its whiteness,
covered better than sleeping eyes."

The night drowned in the simplicity of dawn,
the rooster's cock-a-doodle-doo reaching as far as the morning's horizon,
but before the yolk of the sun emerged
a hand appeared in the dark nest.
The white egg separated from the dark hen. (*From the Sublime*, Tehran, January, 1969)

India

A fat cow
on a lawn as vast as eternity
under a sky as far away as tomorrow;
the left eye: redder than garnet's heart blood.
The other eye: greener than Buddha's solitude.
On the head, as on the shoulders of Zahhak[2]
pines and horns of ivory[3]
on the waist: a litter decorated with a crown;
on the belly: nipple buttons all over,
the udder: full of milk, with nipples pressed together,
the milk flowing towards the expanse of the sea,
one leg, in the enclosure of a snake's coils
the other leg, diseased, swarming with ants.
Its picture in the waves of the defiled river:
a purulent scar gushing out from the earth's liver. (*False Dawn*, November 1977)

Tehran and I

Every morning
when the wet and dry tongues of leaves
inflamed by the sudden sting of the sun bee,
Tehran, the old worm,
opens eyes in a cocoon spun by smog silk
feeling a chronic pain in its heart.

Every noon
when the feverish tongues of leaves
taste the sun's acrid wine
I faint
like an old worm
in a cocoon spun by the silk of imagination,
an unsaid poem inflames in my heart! (*The Sun's Kohl,* Tehran, July 27, 1959)

Notes

1. In Persian, *negâh* 'glance' and *mâh* 'moon' rhyme.
2. A mythical Iranian king on whose two shoulders two serpents had grown and the blood of a young man was needed to quench their thirst. A symbol of lust for power at all costs. Probably, the two arms that are agents of murders have been imagined as two snakes. His name derives from 'dragon' and 'snake' as well.
3. A pun on the Persian words *kâj* 'pine,' *âj* 'ivory,' and *tâj* 'crown.'

Chapter 5

Literary Translation in Modern Times

This chapter makes an attempt to study obstacles on the way of translating Naderpour. The problems are more or less common in all literary translations, but in a rapidly changing world, approaches can be adjusted to meet modern needs. The present chapter, in the way of a memoir, recounts personal experiences of co-translating an outstanding modern Persian poet into English. To be an effective translator, one should know not only two languages but also two cultures. In practice this has posed problems, as one might not be familiar with both source and target cultures or one might simply forget about the nuances of the two during the act of translation. In this chapter it is suggested that when there are two translators with two intercrossing cultural and linguistic backgrounds, the resulting translation will be far richer than when the text is translated single-handedly. Thus, this chapter will invite would-be translators to get involved in a comparable collaborative process.

As a teacher of English literature in Iran who has conducted literary translation courses, I (Rouhollah) have had hard times with my Iranian students translating from their native language (Persian) into English.

They usually fail to transfer not only the connotations of words but also the overall mood or the spirit of poems. This is often the case with famous Persian poets already translated even by native speakers of English. Looking for the roots of the problem, I came across semantic and cultural issues that usually pose problems. However, in practice, it turns out that a single-handed act of translation cannot guarantee success. That is why there are translation workshops. The choice of a colleague to collaborate with is as important as the choice of the literary piece for translation. So how can an ideal collaboration go on? This came about when I met an Iranian-American poet and translator, Dr. Roger Sedarat, on a panel at a translation conference in Stirling, Scotland, in 2008. We were presenting papers on Hafez, the great classical Persian poet. After discovering each other's mutual admiration for Persian and American literature, we decided to collaborate on a modern Persian poet, opting for Nader Naderpour for various reasons. Many of our translations have appeared in English literary journals.

Translation: Alone or Together?

Translation is one of those fields that greatly benefits from collaboration. This is not the case with composing a poem, as the mind of the reader cannot think simultaneously of two minds in the poem while he or she is reading. However, the same reader does not think of how many people have been at work rendering it from another language, as the translator seems invisible. Again he or she will think of one mentality, that is, the poet. Now if there is only one translator, because of the limitation of vocabulary or simply the presence of mind to recall the best equivalent for a word or expression, the poem will be a different one in translation. The result is that the reader either does not notice that the original poem has become something else or he might think that he has been reading a weak poem whose poet is responsible for the error. The internet provides the same facilities for joint translation as paying your bills online instead of physically going to the bank. So time and energy are saved. However, things are not as easy as they might look at first. Much more time can be saved if the two translators are sitting side by side translating, though obviously only if they are living or working close to each other, not in two different parts of the world. Another issue is that they might not be free or in the mood (which is a necessary element in literary translation) simultaneously. So the edited translation remains in the box of the fellow translator to be dealt with at a convenient time.

WHY NADER NADERPOUR?

The subjects a modern poet like Naderpour deals with is more perceptible by a contemporary translator than one who might translate him a couple of centuries later. The same is true of classical Persian poets. If they were translated in the fourteenth century there might have been fewer problems than now, as one has to be familiar with many literary, cultural, sociological and historical issues of the time.

Naderpour is a poet less known in the English speaking world. He is a poet whose sensitivities can evoke forgotten memories in everyone's mind. He speaks in a language familiar to us through the universal themes of nature, romance, eroticism, passage of time: youth, old age, and death. Because his poems were written over the course of decades and cover a variety of subjects, it is hard to pigeonhole him in just one school of poetry or one generation of poets. We believe that there was also something about Naderpour's ability to get so close to nature, a somewhat refreshing return to the romantic in what has become in America such a post-modern, surrealistic time for poetry. As far as modern Persian poets go, Naderpour proved a somewhat easy choice, as he remains relatively unknown in the west and the poetry from his last books have failed to appear in a complete English translation.

The Preliminaries

The choice of our subject was not easy, as we had to consider at least three main factors: the novelty of the work, which implied being unknown or little known in the target language; the literary merit of the work, and the taste of the audience. So I started looking for a poet who could meet the demands. I chose Naderpour. A few poems were sent to Roger, and we quickly noticed we had found the poet we were looking for. There has been only one book on him in English, *False Dawn: Persian Poems by Nader Naderpour* (1986) by Professor Michael Craig Hillmann, while Naderpour was alive and the poetry from his last books (arguably his best), had yet to come out. We had a sense that we were both able to surrender to this poet's voice, allowing him to speak through us, both in Persian and English.

Our process insured accuracy along with the literary spirit of the original. I am fairly familiar with Persian and English literature and Roger had the advantage of being an Iranian-American poet writing and translating in English as well. Our back and forth email process provided us with fresh ways of considering the poems as we drafted and redrafted new versions for each other.

Poems in Process

The poems chosen to typify Naderpour were naturally from all subject categories, some of which have been reproduced here. The problems encountered have been introduced as well. They have been from various fields but typical ones will be discussed here.

In a poem addressed to the Caspian Sea the poet describes the sea in various terms. The epithets employed set up various imagery: semantic, cultural, literary and so on. So in each case we had to readjust our position to keep up the mood, the spirit, and the beauty of the poem while having an eye on the taste and sensibility of the audience in the English speaking world. Consider that the footnotes provided here are from the first take and different from the final version.

1. "Petition" or "Apostrophe" or "A Modest Address"

You fluent green!
You impossible simplicity!

You whose wave of Persian letters makes every dot a bird!

You rising meter of the moon's rhyme!
You mainstay of the moon's rhyme!
You sign of smooth and easeful expression!
You sea, a body of metrical waters!
You sea, a form but two meanings[1]

You Dome, you Rome!
You Sassanid monument in Kermanshah!

You deep, you high, you dread, you threat,
you green, you Caspian Sea!

In the first and second lines the images come from two literary figures from Persian literature. In the translation, the word 'eloquent' somehow suggests the source of the thought, but in the second line 'impossible simplicity' does not show that it is a literary trope. Thus something goes missing in the translation. 'Impossible simplicity' might not bring to the mind of the reader that this is a style of writing. So a footnote might be of help.

A word-for-word translation of line seven, "You whose wave of Persian letters makes every dot a bird!" reads like this: 'You on whose letters of waves every bird is a dot.' The word "Persian" has been added to make it clear that dots are meaningful in Persian alphabet. Thus a constant reference to Persian language and poetry forms the fabric of the imagery.

The most difficult parts have been those that were heavily reliant on Persian language vocabulary. A line in "The Capsized Sun," which was most challenging, included a play on the three words of *qâyeq* 'boat,' *haqâyeq* 'facts, truth,' and *shaqâyeq* 'anemone.' So puns and multiple meanings were our most formidable obstacles.

2 . The Capsized Sun

2.1. Take 1

Like a woman closing windows one by one and turning off the light
Night extinguished the stars and went to bed

The red in the white dawn's sky
Painted crimson flowers on milk waterfall
Some wind, expounded the green book of trees
Then fire flourished in the silk of the grass.
It was not fire,
On the green sea, it was a boat.
*The sun was truth capsized.
Or it was the explosion of a Darkness Complex
In anemone's red sun.

*Roger, I wonder how meaningful the play on *qâyeq*, *haqâyeq*, and *shaqâyeq* will be. I really cannot make much sense out of them.

2.2. Take 2

The sun was capsized truth.
Or the explosion of a darkness complex
In a solar red anemone.

2.3. Take 3

Then fire flourished in the silky grass.
Not a real fire
on the green sea,
a boat
capsizing the sun.

2.4. Take 4

Regarding the problem with "Capsized Sun" and the play on *shaqâyeq, qâyeq*, and *haqâyeq*: In Persian there is a famous line about some poets: "When stretched for rhyme/ the poet will veer to nonsense." The reverse is also true. The poet might already have had certain rhyming words in mind but is forcibly relating them. The problem with "The Capsized Sun" might be this. So we should not worry too much about them.

2.5. Take 5

(Rouhollah:) "I decided to have another look at the matter although I still think the poet is in sweat to yoke dissimilar things together. It seems distorted facts put by darkness now make more sense:

'The capsized sun was telling (i.e. facts were distorted like a capsized sun),'

Or

'the capsized sun was the reality
It was the outburst of darkness
In the red radiance of anemone.'"

3. Prayer at Sunrise

Red-skinned Indian,
how do you feel on a polar night?
Has the chilling silence
driven you to sleep?
Or has oblivion blotted out
the cold reality of past white days?

Can't you recall
those August afternoons
when a violet cackle
beamed from your mouth,
the gold fire of your breath
burning earth and heaven?

In the original the red-Indian has a gold-filmed tooth which sparkles as he laughs. This became a point of debate as we noticed in our two cultures two different classes of people usually have their teeth gold-filmed. So the problem was resolved by actually approaching the point indirectly.

> 4. The Last Supper
>
> "With the rough immoral stone,
> at the enemy's infernal gallows,
> we bruised Hallaj who shouted the truth.
> we transferred power from our saints to Yazid;
> we, more pious than all the impure,
> dipped nails into the friend's blood."

"The Last Supper" is replete with cultural points. So, either we had to go round them or provide footnote comments to which I refer the reader to the third chapter in this book.

Achievements of Joint Translation

A point usually less noticed is the role of personal relationships in joint translations. At the beginning we were not only tackling poems and hence the poet but also, quite unknowingly, our co-translator. So, more energy was exerted for initial poems. As we carried on we sensed that we were proceeding more easily, one reason being that we were getting more and more familiar with the poet and also our translating partner, his taste, cast of mind, and worldview. Thus, translating was delving into the personality recesses not only of the poet but of each other. We gradually took these issues into consideration while translating.

Another benefit of joint translation has been the enrichment of teaching experience. Collaboration with Professor Roger Sedarat, a native speaker of English, has given me the opportunity to show my students my own initial translations and the final jointly translated versions. This has been a unique chance of enhancing the quality of literary translation. The experience of co-translation has more advantages than disadvantages. When there is no possibility of living in two cultures, there is little chance of knowing both well enough. The solution offered in this paper is one effective and economical way to know about people via translation. It is the good luck of modern scholars to live in an age when the internet offers help in matters like literary translation.

Notes

1. See the discussion in the third chapter, Part 3: Lost Land.

Epilogue

This book is about the poet, not his co-translators. So, instead of summarizing what we have already said, we intend to recapitulate what Naderpour has been saying in his own way. As a poet, he defines himself, what he is and would be, and the world in the language of poetry. The following poem is in fact the sum of all the poems we have presented.

   The Poet

   A man lives in the mirror,
   reflecting blue
   with imagined sunlight.

   From the smoky sky
   he extracts the fiery morning
   and with his lamp
   he captures the night.

   A creator of spring,
   he raises green thoughts
   stemming from pure soil
   to scaffolding of bright horizons,
   then lowers them with the sun.

   He sees through capillaries
   to the sap of life,
   the meandering circulation
   of the ebb and flow.

   In his almighty hand
   he holds the restless
   cosmic pulses
   like tiny pearl beads,

interpreting all motion.

He writes the garnet's story
of its blood-red formation
in the calcareous womb
or the fate of the shell's love
from its germination
in the sand grain
to its birth in the pearl.
He inscribes love's alchemy[1]
upon the metal plate
of bright burning
destiny.

A man lives in the mirror,
interpreting eternity
between indecipherable lines
of wrinkled skin and broken glass. (*The Last Supper*, Tehran, February 18, 1973)

Notes

1. In Persian *mehr* 'love' and *mohr* 'stamp' are spelled the same.

Bibliography

Alishan, Leonardo. "Naqd-o Barresiye Sobhe Dorûghin" ("An Analysis of *False Dawn*." Eidgah 350–362.

Barahani, Reza. "Tasvirgari Bozorg" ("A Great Imagist"). Salahshour 61–71.

Behbahini, Simin. *Yâde Ba'zi Nafârât (In Memory of Some People)*. Tehran: Alborz, 1999.

Eidgah Torqabe'i, Vahid, ed., *Kohan Diârâ: Naghd-o Tahlil-e Ash'âr-e Nâder Nâderpûr (My Ancient Land: An Analysis of Nader Naderpour's Poetry)*. Tehran: Sokhan, 2009.

Farzan, Massud, "Contemporary Poetry in Iran." Yarshater, *Persian* 336–66.

Hillmann, Michael Craig. *False Dawn: Persian Poems*. Austin, Tex: The Dep. of Oriental and African Languages and Literatures. The University of Texas at Austin, 1986.

Hoqouqi, Mohammad. *Sher-o Shâerân (Poetry and Poets)*. Tehran: Negah, 1389.

Karimi-Hakkak, Ahmad. "Nader Naderpour." Mozaffari and Karimi-Hakkak 395-98.

Mozaffari, Nahid and Ahmad Karimi-Hakkak, eds. *Strange Times, My Dear: The Pen Anthology of Contemporary Iranian Literature*. New York: Arcade, 2005.

Naderpour, Nader. "Goft-o-gûy'ee ba Nâder Nâderpûr: Shâ'er-e Bozorg-e Moâser-e Iran" ("An Interview with Nader Naderpour: The Great Contemporary Iranian Poet"). *Mirâse Iran (Persian Heritage)* 4:15 (Fall 1999): 114–117.

Roya'ee, Yadollah. "Ta'amoli bar Sher-e Moâser ba Gozari az Kârhâye Nâderpûr ("Contemplating Contemporary Poetry with a Reference to Naderpour's Works"). Eidgah 213–255.

Roya'ee, Yadollah. *Halâk-e-Aghl be Vaght-e-Andishidan* (*Absent-mindedness at the Time of Thinking*). Tehran: Morvarid, 1978.

Salahshour, Yazdan. *Dar Âyeneh: Naghd-o Barrasye She'r-e Nâder Nâderpûr* (*In Mirror: An Analysis of Nader Naderpour's Poetry*). Tehran: Morvarid, 2001.

Shafi'ee Kadakani, Mohammad Reza. A*dvâr-e She'r-e Fârsi az Mashroutiat ta Soghoute-e Saltanat* (*The History of Persian Poetry from the Constitutional Revolution to the End of Monarchy*). Tehran: Sokhan, 2001.

Shakki, Hossein. "Taghazzol va Âsheqâneh-sarâ'i dar Âsâre Nâder Nâderpûr" (Lyricism and Romanticism in Nader Naderpour). *Hafiz Monthly* 33 (August 2006): 73-78.

Shams Langroodi (M. T. J. Gilani). *Târikhe Tahlilie She're No* (*An Analytical History of Persian Modern Poetry*). Vol. 2. Tehran: Nashre Markaz, 1991.

Yarshater, Ehsan. "A Star Ceases to Shine," *Persica* 17 (2001): 137-53.

Yarshater, Ehsan, ed. *Persian Literature*. New York: State University of New York Press, 1988.

Zarqani, Mahdi. *Morûri bar Daftarhâye She'r-e Nâderpûr* (*A Survey of Naderpour's Books of Poems*). Eidgah 331–349.

www.ingramcontent.com/pod-product-compliance
Lightning Source LLC
Chambersburg PA
CBHW030557230426
43661CB00054B/2164